What You're Hiding *is* Hindering *Your Blessings*

Tina Bailey

Rain Publishing
KNIGHTDALE, NORTH CAROLINA

Copyright © 2013 by **Tina Bailey**.

All rights reserved. No part of this publication may be reproduced, distributed or transmitted in any form or by any means, including photocopying, recording, or other electronic or mechanical methods, without the prior written permission of the publisher, except in the case of brief quotations embodied in critical reviews and certain other noncommercial uses permitted by copyright law. For permission requests, write to the publisher, addressed "Attention: Permissions Coordinator," at the address below.

Tina Bailey/Rain Publishing
PO Box 702
Knightdale, NC 27545
www.rainpublishing.com

Book Cover Design and Layout: Trevis C. Bailey, www.SDCreativeWorks.com
Edited by: Rain Publishing, LLC;
www.RainPublishing.com

Ordering Information: Quantity sales. Special discounts are available on quantity purchases by corporations, associations, and others. For details, contact the "Special Sales Department" at the address above.

What You're Hiding is Hindering Your Blessings/ Tina Bailey. —1st ed.
ISBN: 978-0-9916618-1-7
Library of Congress: 2014936245

Acknowledgements

To God for giving me the strength to work through my personal struggles and drawing me closer to You in the process.

To my husband for allowing me to be transparent and use our struggles to help others.

To my children Chaz, Cynthia, Sedrick, Yvonne, and Tyler: Thank you for the unconditional love that only children can provide, for helping me see the good in me when I couldn't see it in myself, for loving me just as I am.

To my mom for your continued love and allowing me to make my own decisions in life.

To my girlfriends, Sabrina, Cynthia and Brandy, thanks for providing me words of encouragement, wisdom, and even tough love when I needed it. You guys provide a support system like no other.

To my Aunt Teresa you have always been my inspiration but your support during this season in my life has been extraordinary. It was your loving words that helped me to learn compassion. You have helped me so tremendously on this path of healing and deliverance and words cannot begin to express how thankful I am for the part in which you played. May God continue to bless you.

To all those who have been a part of my continued growth during this process, I say thank you! Whether you provided me with encouragement, motivation or even a hurdle to jump – I thank God for you because it was an opportunity for me to grow.

CONTENTS

Trying to Fit In 1
Looking For Love 11
A Form of Love 19
My Secret Lover 31
But My Vows 41
The Dream 49
Will the Real You Stand up? 55
Life Begins Now 63
You can Lead a Horse to Water 67
Carry Your Own Cross 75
The Strength to Let Go 83
Loving Me Is Okay 91
Just a Little Better 95
    ABOUT THE AUTHOR 97

Introduction

Life is a precious gift given to us by God. He gives us the opportunity to go out in to the world He created for us and enjoy the abundance. I have learned that our gift to Him is what we do with our lives but unfortunately we often become caught up in things that do not really matter. I believe in having a direction for your life. Benjamin Franklin put it best – "if you fail to plan you plan to fail."

I've always thought I had a plan for my life, but what I quickly realized is that plans change and if you are not willing to follow suit you will get lost in the shuffle of it all. This book discusses the tragedy of not being willing to deter from the plan or reexamine the plan you have for your life. I never had a desire to write about the things I experienced but God has a way of making you do those things you never desired to do. Now I can see purpose in every aspect of my life. This book will help you surrender the guilt associated with the things in your past and transform your story into a blessing for you and those who come into your life.

Dear God,
It is my prayer that the individuals reading this book will see that they are loved and they are exactly where they need to be in this journey called Life. God, help us all remember that You will never put more on us than we can bear and that You will provide everything we need in order to be successful on this journey. Father, I pray the lessons that I have been able to experience will help prevent someone else from experiencing the same hurt or at least be able to give them the strength they will need to reach the next level. I ask You now to open their

minds and their hearts to use the experiences of life to grow and help someone else with their testimony of how You have brought them through. God, help them to understand that they are more than a conqueror and that You have already given them the victory- if they would only walk in their deliverance. In Jesus' Name I pray.

Trying to Fit In

> "Happiness is like a butterfly which, when pursued, is always beyond our grasp, but, if you will sit down quietly, may alight upon you." ~Nathaniel Hawthorne

> "Love is to let those we love be perfectly themselves, and not to twist them to fit our own image... otherwise we love only the reflection of ourselves we find in them." ~Author Unknown

A square has straight lines with defined ends and beginnings, where a circle has one continuous line that never ends. If you attempt to roll a square it will land on each of its sides and require you to push it again. However if you roll a circle, it will continue to roll until it is stopped by another object. A square will never fit perfectly inside of a circle. The two just don't match. If you find a circle large enough to hold the square, there are empty spaces that will surround it. If the circle is too small, you will find the corners of the square will lie outside of the circumference of the circle.

Growing up it seemed that I never really fit into any of the circles of life. As a young girl, I found myself constantly trying to fit in with one group or another only to be shunned away and made to feel less than. I was told I was too nerdy to be with the cool kids and not quite smart enough to be with the bright kids.

I can remember being the only African American in my Math and English classes when it was not cool for that to happen, and my peers would say cruel things to me. I was always told I thought I was better than everyone else or called an Uncle Tom because of my classes and my grades. It didn't matter that I was in those classes or made those grades because I studied and applied myself. In the eyes of my peers, it was because I thought I was better, yet deep inside myself, I just wanted to be like everyone else and to be liked by everyone. I remember deliberately making bad grades in class or ignoring the fact that I knew the answers to the questions proposed by the teacher so I wouldn't be called a nerd or be picked on by my peers for being smart. I despised being different.

It's amazing how certain memories can bring back some of the most horrific feelings. I remember being in class one day and the teacher asked a question that I clearly knew the answer to. I sat still and watched as so many wrong answers were given. My teacher looked at me and called my name. I kindly looked at her and said, "I don't know." After class she asked me to stay because she wanted to talk to me. I will never forget the words she spoke. She told me that I was one of her brightest students, however I was allowing my fear of being different to hold me back from what I was called to accomplish. At the time, I did not receive what she said and it was not until later in life that I really understood what she was trying to get me to see. I was different and it was okay.

I did not feel that I was capable of being successful and pursuing my dreams. My dreams were extraordinary. They were big! They were unheard of. Most importantly, I had never seen anyone in my community accomplish the things that I dreamed of, like having a happy life, a successful life, a prosperous life. It seemed no one from my community went on to be a doctor, lawyer or business owner. They just lived a normal life. Most of the families appeared to be dysfunctional and broken. Many of the kids were raised in single parent homes. It is funny how distorted your memories can be when you do not want to see them any other way.

I grew up in a small town with limited resources. We were bused out of my community to a town that was predominately white for school. There was another community of African American children who were also bused to this school. These individuals were from what we considered the rough side of town. Because of the reputation associated with them, each of the African American students in our school were deemed to be cut from the same cloth. Some of the children from my community began to act like these individuals, possibly because that was what was expected of them from those in authority or maybe because they were just trying to fit in. Most of us remained true to our upbringing and stayed clear of the turmoil associated with the others. Those of us who did not intermingle with the other group were considered even by them as different.

At home in my small community there was a limited number of girls my age to play with so I ran and played with the boys. Although I wasn't as fast or strong as them, I gave it my all and found fun in doing so. Yet soon the boys were tired of having to wait on me and would run off and play their own games. When the boys would leave, I would climb in the trees and play with my Barbie dolls. My grandmother would call me the "little prissy tomboy." She would always tell me that I was different and that it was okay, but again I didn't want to be different. I just wanted to fit in with someone somewhere.

It seems as though I've struggled all my life to be accepted and be what I thought everyone else wanted me to be or what I thought everyone needed me to be. I wanted to be the perfect daughter, the perfect sister, the perfect friend, the perfect student and then the perfect wife, perfect mother, perfect employee and the perfect Christian but what I failed to realize is that there is no perfection in this world.

While trying to be everything for everyone else or at least trying to be what I thought they needed me to be, I lost sight of who I was and what I wanted out of life. I can think of times when I smiled and laughed but it's difficult to remember a time when I was genuinely happy and content with my life. It seemed I always put up a front and acted like everything was okay and that my world was great. I found the easiest way was to hide in the background and allow everything and everyone else to shine.

As a student, I can remember one of my teachers telling me, "You are not presenting your best work." It's so clear now that she was telling the truth, but at the time, I felt I was giving all I needed to give. I felt that anything more would not be accepted and it would be a waste of my time. What actually happened was I began to withdraw even more. I shut down and stayed that way through most of my adult life. I knew how to put on a front to accomplish the task placed before me, but I resented every moment. I even took for granted the opportunities I was given by only doing the minimum or not accepting the opportunities at all.

For example, being presented with an opportunity to run for student council caused panic attacks in my mind. The idea of being in front of others and being judged by my peers was something I didn't feel I could deal with. Although I believed in the people who were encouraging me to take on this task, I didn't believe in my own abilities to perform at the level they thought I could. Instead of running for an office, I worked the campaign for a classmate and she won. Working the background became a norm for me. It quickly became the way I viewed and lived my life. When things appeared too hard or too much of a challenge, I would shut down and retreat to a more comfortable setting, a place where I could not be seen.

Finding a place of comfort or a place to hide became an easy task. When presented with any type of conflict or obstacle, I found I just accepted that it was the way things were supposed to be and not a part of my destiny. I couldn't see that it was just preparation for what was to come. When things became uncomfortable, I saw it as a sign that I was headed in the wrong direction instead of an opportunity to grow. I had become accustomed to not fitting in, so making myself invisible shielded me from accepting that I was not a part. I realize now that I was more than a part. I was being prepared for greatness. I was being prepared for an opportunity to help others come out of their shells and allow their real selves to shine.

I was a square trying to fit into a circle's world. I was different at a time in my life when I did not want to be different. Then God spoke to me and showed me He wanted to use my differences to make a difference in this world. It was time for me to reveal my true self and begin a process of healing and deliverance. Now it is time to allow God to use my experiences to help others who are struggling with the pain of wanting to fit in and all the choices that go along with it.

In school we all had to endure Physical Education. Some of us enjoyed it more than others and I was one of those who actually hated PE. I had to display my weakness in front of my peers and prove that I wasn't good at something. I couldn't climb the ropes, I couldn't straddle that gosh darn horse, and I couldn't do a back flip. What I was good at, was keeping scores and stats, so I began to gravitate to track and field and became instrumental to the coaches in that area. Even so, the day came when we were presented with jumping hurdles. In order to participate in track and field you had to try every component of the sport. The thought of jumping hurdles gives me a headache even today and makes me want to roll over and die, but looking back at that period, I have determined that life is like running on a track full of hurdles.

When we were first introduced to the hurdles, they were set at the lowest height possible. As we began to master those, they were raised slightly to cause us to try even harder. This continued until the coach felt we reached our potential; yet a good coach would continue to push his student to take a chance on the next height. During those times of growth, several things can happen; you can clear the hurdle, you can knock the hurdle over, or you can fall flat on your face. The main thing you have to remember is you must get back up and keep running.

When you are faced with a hurdle that has been knocked down, it can cause you to lose your balance and cause you to stumble, but it should not take you out of the race. When you are running and you knock the hurdle down and fall, the first thing your coach will say is get up and try it again. There are many reasons for this. If you remain laying on the ground, not only do you take the chance of being stomped by those coming behind you, but you allow yourself to stay in a defeated position. The same thing applies to life. There are going to be things that cause you to stumble and lose your balance. There may even be situations that cause you to fall flat on your face, yet you cannot allow those things to take you out of your race. Each hurdle you clear was because of preparation and determination. As you clear hurdles, there is great joy in your accomplishment, but you cannot allow that temporary satisfaction to become so relevant that you forget the remaining stretch of the course. You must use that triumph to help you prepare for the next. As you are running, your focus must be on the next hurdle, not on the one that you just jumped. Even if you knock it down or fall in the process you must complete the race.

Many people get caught up in seeing the flickering lights of the finish line and become distracted. However, in life, the finish line is death. You are going to hit hurdles and obstacles as long as you stay on this earth. It is up to you to determine how to use these hurdles to prepare you for the next jump. During all those times that I didn't feel I fit in or that my best was not good enough, I was being prepared for the race of my life. It was learning to jump those hurdles and understanding the purpose of jumping those hurdles that helped me continue the race.

I can clearly remember the moment a feeling of defeat set in. I was sitting in my room and felt like I had lost every desire to breathe and every desire to exist but it was as if God Himself reached down and reminded me of my fight and victory over those hurdles. I realized I had a choice, I could lay flat on my face and get stomped on or I could rise to the occasion, brush myself off, figure out what I did wrong that caused me to fall in the first place, and start running again. That is exactly what I did.

There was a season of my life where I was attacked physically, mentally, verbally, and emotionally and believed that for some reason, I deserved each and every one of those attacks. It was as if I felt this was the way life was supposed to be and that I had to endure it, that it was all for some reason and a purpose. After considerable searching, praying and truly seeking God, I realized that not only had I stopped pursuing the purpose He had placed within me; I had lost sight of who He was in my life. I began to pursue the desires of man instead of the desires of God. I began to crave the voice and approval of man and it became so loud that God's voice became part of the background and eventually faded away.

Although God is too much of a gentleman to force Himself on you, He will make subtle attempts to get your attention. With me, it was removing those things that I had placed before Him and seeing Him bless me anyway. God is just good like that. During the times when I should have failed, He carried me, the times when I felt like giving up, He reminded me of my purpose, the times when I found myself crying, He wiped my tears and rocked me until I was able to continue on.

When people did not understand why I did the things I did, God showed me why I was doing them. I've learned that He loves me too much to allow a hurdle to knock me out of the race. Many times we will not fit in with the group, because that's not the group God wants us to be a part of. Many times it will seem impossible to jump that hurdle, but that's when you have to dig deep and allow God to lift you above it. God desires the best for you. He does not demand perfection, just faith in Him to see you through the rough spots. There will be times even after you've made this declaration that you will fall into the old ways of before. You may even find yourself not wanting to jump any more hurdles and just give up. That is when you reach deep inside yourself and ask God to help you through. His faithfulness and love will bring you through every time.

Apply It

Focus on a time in your life where you changed or masked who you were in order to fit into the group, or when you did not give your best because you had already determined that it would not be accepted. Think of a time when you wanted to give up and end the race but something on the inside would not allow you to quit. That was God speaking to you. He knows what you can do and what requires a little more time to accomplish. God will never leave you in a situation without help. He knows that we require encouragement and support from outside forces. Do not take for granted those people who spoke into your life, they were not placed there by accident. They spoke into the inner core of your being and gave you strength that you weren't even aware of. Give thanks for those moments when you wanted to give up and something on the inside would not allow you. Everything happens for a reason. Each trial and tribulation that you've experienced has been designed just for you, to strengthen you. Be grateful for the lessons learned. Write a letter to yourself forgiving yourself for not being the real you and for allowing someone else's view of who you are to cloud the view of who you are destined to be.

Dear God,

Help me to see that I am fearfully and wonderfully made (Psalms 139:14). Help me to see that You instilled in me dreams, hopes, and desires that I may be able to live a purpose-filled life and help those that desire to be more. God help me to use the opportunities of this season to grow and be what You desire me to be. In Jesus' Name I pray.

Looking For Love

> *"Unhappiness is not knowing what we want and killing ourselves to get it."* ~Don Herold
>
> *"The hunger for love is much more difficult to remove than the hunger for bread."* ~Mother Teresa

Love has been defined as a passionate tender feeling towards someone. Another definition is a desire to satisfy the needs of a person, withholding nothing from them. A mother can feel love for her child before he or she is even born. She makes sacrifices to bring this life into the world, nurturing him or her from the inside out. Love is an emotion that every person is born with, yet is not cultivated in everyone. When a baby is born, it is love that helps that child to grow and mature. A lack of love and affection can distort the way that child views love and him/herself. It is love that allows a person to attempt to love an unlovable person. It is the desire for love that makes you sacrifice your own happiness for the happiness of someone else. It is love that blinds you from all the hatred in the world. It is love that makes you vulnerable yet stronger than the deepest hurts. It is a lack of love that can cause people to do the worst things imaginable. It is love that keeps a person in a destructive relationship.

Every person in this world desires to be loved, yet every person in this world does not know how to show love. We are taught how to express love at an early age. We also learn what things are unlovable and unacceptable. There should never be a moment when a person feels unloved, however it is experienced everyday by many people. That feeling of being unloved has caused people to gravitate toward things that can cause them harm. It is amazing to me that the feeling of being unloved was set early in my life. I did not understand why I felt unloved. I knew that my parents loved me. I knew my grandmother and aunts loved me. They expressed it in some form every day. Growing up we had a tradition of going to my grandmother's house every night before going to bed. I loved to lie in her arms and hear her tell me that she loved me and that I was special. It was her unconditional acceptance of me that taught me how to love others. I was good at showing everyone else love but did not feel that I deserved love or that it was acceptable to love myself. I had so many flaws and in my eyes, I lacked character.

My father was another person who showed me a view of unconditional love. A father provides love and protection from everything. At least that's what I remember from my father. I remember growing up hearing of how he drank a lot, cursed a lot, and could be mean and rowdy. Yet the man I remember was kind, generous, and protective. Yes I remember times I would pass the local liquor store and my dad's car would be there, but I never saw him drink anything. I never heard him disrespect anyone. Regardless of what he was doing, he always had time for me. My parents never married each other but I remember the love they had for each other. My mother even told me my dad was her first love. She knew him from when she was younger but she moved away and married another man. That marriage was full of physical altercations and a lot of verbal abuse. It was my dad who went and encouraged her to leave the relationship and move back home. I believe it was her marriage and the streets of Brooklyn that stripped my mother from her ability to show physical love and affection. One of the memories I have from my childhood is seeing my mom and dad dance. He would twirl her around and she would laugh. When he came into the room she would smile and seemed happy, a happiness that I didn't get a chance to see every day. My mom was one of those individuals who took care of everyone else's needs and not her own. As a single parent, she worked two jobs at times and was always tired. My mother taught me that her love was shown in the things that she provided for us. The things she did for us was her demonstration of love. Because she did not use many words of affection, we grew not to expect many.

My father always seemed so different in comparison to my mother. One Saturday, arrangements had been made for me to spend the weekend with him. When he came to pick me up, I was doing the normal thing of running and playing with the boys. My mother called me into the house to start my bath. I did and left the water running in the tub. Water was all over the floor. Now, I can count the times on one hand that I was physically punished by my mother, yet a punishment was definitely in order for this event. When mom went to discipline me, my dear dad stepped in and convinced her that it was not necessary. He even jumped in front of the belt to keep her from hitting me with it. He did everything in his power to convince her that I would never do it again. It was at that time that I associated protection with love. However, my father died when

I was nine years old. It seems from that time forward, I was looking for someone to replace the love and attention that a young girl could only get from her father. I wanted to be loved like that again. I would do anything just to feel that type of love and protection.

My father's death left me stoic and emotionless for years. My grandmother's love was the only thing that seemed to penetrate the walls I had built up. She accepted me just as I was. She didn't push, she didn't judge. She just loved me, but it wasn't the same as a father's love. In high school, when one of the most popular boys in the school began to notice me, it only made sense that I would take hold with no intention of letting go. He was two grades ahead of me in school and it seemed every girl wanted to be his girlfriend. Considered the "bookworm" of the group or the church girl, what could he possibly see in me? When I learned that he was considering asking me out on a date, it didn't matter that it was because of a dare made between him and his friends as to whether or not he could get me to go out on a date with him. The mere thought that he had chosen me was all that mattered. The dare was not one-sided, however. He was dating this other girl who for some reason didn't like me and she made it known. After an altercation in the hallway, I kindly informed her that I would be with "her man" the next day. Already knowing that he had shown interest, I knew I could make that happen. It didn't matter that he wasn't my type – truly because I didn't know what my type was. All I knew was he was showing me attention and I liked it.

When I got pregnant at seventeen, I was sure that it was a part of my destiny. This was the way it was supposed to be. I can remember telling my mom, "he loves me so much, he gave me a baby." I remember feeling that finally I would have someone who loved me unconditionally. I would have someone who needed me. There would finally be someone who would never leave me. I had found my purpose in life. I was to be a mother. Four years later the next baby came and I began forming the image in my mind of what things were supposed to look like – the big house with the white picket fence, the kids running around with smiles on their faces, a hot meal on the table every day when the husband came home from work, a house so immaculate and peaceful that people came by just to relax, a life that people lived in awe of. I didn't need anyone or anything else, I had it all.

I was creating a masterpiece. I knew what everything was supposed to look like, I knew how it was supposed to feel, I knew exactly what I was doing until one day it all shattered. I remember feeling not only was I not going to be able to finish this masterpiece that I had worked so hard to create, but that it was all a deluded fantasy. The greens didn't seem green anymore, the blues had turned black and nothing really mattered. The masterpiece could not be finished; it seemed as though someone had stolen my crayons. I found myself asking God to remove me – maybe I was the problem. I only believed I was happy if everyone around me was happy. My way of being loved was by giving love. I didn't need anything in return, or so I thought. I believed it was my job, my destiny, to make everyone happy. I was taught that a woman is to be submissive to her husband, to love him unconditionally and want what is best for him at all costs. Therefore if my family, any member of my family, was not happy it had to be because of something I was or wasn't doing.

I was searching for a man to give me the love that only God Himself could give me, that unconditional, unbiased love. I remember sitting down writing a letter to God, expressing all the issues I had with Him and how He had let me down. I told Him about the masterpiece I was working on and how it was now gone. I told Him about all the work I had done for Him and that I was angry He had allowed this to happen to me. I told Him how disappointed I was in Him for not taking me out of the equation before it got to this point. I was angry! After completing my letter, I cried myself to sleep. The next morning I woke up and saw the letter I had written. I laughed at myself and tore the letter up. I then wrote a letter asking God to forgive me for blaming Him for decisions that I made without consulting Him. Then I laid quietly and took a few deep breaths and allowed myself to rest in God's arms. It was then, that I finally felt the love I had desperately longed for, that unconditional acceptance of another person.

At the beginning of time, God showed His love towards mankind by providing us with everything we could physically need. However, He desires that we seek Him for our emotional and spiritual needs as well. It took me a long time to realize that no man could love me like God does and even longer to realize that I deserved to be loved. The masterpiece of life is not what others think of you, but what God thinks of you. In the Garden of Eden, Adam and Eve had everything that could be desired by man. It was when they allowed the words of others (satan) to distract them that they began to get lost in the ways of the world. We do the same thing today. We get so consumed with what man thinks about us that we lose sight of what God thinks. When you're going through those moments of feeling unlovable, undesired, unworthy, you need to ask yourself "who told you that?" God said we are fearfully and wonderfully made (Psalms 139:14). We are made in His image (Genesis 1:26). He loved us so much that He allowed His Son to die for us (John 3:16). Why allow anyone to tell you any different?

Our kids are growing up in a society where they are being taught that they are not good enough. They are being lead to believe that their best is not good enough. Our young girls are starving themselves to be skinny. Our young boys are walking around with their pants hanging below their waist trying to make a statement. Gangs are taking over our communities. More jails are being built than colleges. Suicide is now a part of everyday conversation in the schools. Many of our kids can name at least one person they know that has committed suicide or attempted suicide. Being a virgin is viewed as abnormal. Each and every one of these scenarios are cries to be loved and to be accepted. Yet it's hard to teach your children to love themselves when you don't love yourself. Domestic violence is running rapid in our households and no one wants to address it.

It all starts with you. God wants you to have life abundantly and to be loved unconditionally, not superficial love, not love that has stipulations, but love that is pure. First we have to understand that we deserve it before we can obtain it.

Apply It

We can find any reason good or bad to love other people but never ourselves. Sit down and write a love letter to yourself. Speak only of your positive traits physically, mentally, and emotionally. Name them one by one. Show yourself love and adoration. Write all the things you like about yourself. Talk about your accomplishments. No negative talk is allowed. When you have finished writing it, go into a secluded area and read it aloud.

Dear God,

Help me to remember Your Word says for me to love others as I love myself. (John 13:34). I cannot love anyone until I learn to love myself. Help me to see what You see in me. Help me to see the strengths You have placed inside of me and learn to nurture them and love them. I am Your vessel. Help me to remember that. In Jesus' Name I pray.

A Form of Love

> "The minute you settle for less than you deserve, you get even less than you settled for." ~ Maureen Dowd
>
> "If you really put a small value upon yourself, rest assured that the world will not raise your price." ~Author Unknown

Accepting anything less than what you really desire, whether it is a job or a relationship, is settling. God did not design you to settle. Anytime you settle it reflects the nature of your faith: the faith you have in yourself and the faith you have in God. When you do just enough to satisfy a task, it will never give you the full satisfaction you desire. Settling opens up the door for discontentment and hopelessness. Have you ever worked on a project, knowing that you haven't given it your best, and became frustrated when someone commented on what you have done? You tend to see each comment as negativity, unable to see anything positive in their assessment. It is then that the frustration intensifies. Realize that frustration comes from within. It is not the comment of the other person that taunts you; it is your own judgment that constantly nags at you.

Constructive criticism is good; it allows you to get another perspective of what you are working on. It should motivate you to do better, to achieve more. However, when you second guess what you are doing or don't give your best to what you are doing, the constructive criticism highlights all the flaws that you already know exist.

Doing just enough in order to say you have completed the task, is settling. Whether it's getting a passing grade when you are capable of a superior grade, attaching yourself to a person that is emotionally unavailable, submitting that report a few minutes before the deadline or allowing your true dreams to be stifled by your unwillingness to push through the clouds and storms, it is all a form of settling. You were created for better than that; you were created for greatness. The desires in your heart were placed there a long time ago. You were not designed for failure nor were you designed to give up, yet many times you find yourselves accepting any form of your desire as enough.

There will be times when you get tired of fighting through the obstacles and want to give up. It is those times that you need to see the issue for what it really is. It is a lack of belief, trust in yourself and your ability to achieve what it is you truly desire. It also stems from not believing that you deserve what you are pursuing or that you can have it. It is so easy to provide words of encouragement to others and motivate them to strive for the best, yet when it comes to your own situations, those words just aren't there or don't seem to be enough. That's when you have to look outside of yourself and ask for help. You have to ask God to send people who can help you through this storm.

Think of a pilot flying a plane through a storm. He is informed during his training that should he ever get into an uncontrollable situation, he is to contact the main tower for instruction. Although he is aware of the tower staff's existence, he will not know the magnitude of their abilities until he is placed in a situation where their assistance is required. The true essence of his training is not how well he can manipulate the plane through the storm, it is his ability to reach out to the main tower for assistance and follow their instructions. Contacting the main tower for assistance does not make him a bad pilot. Quite the opposite, it makes him a very skilled and smart pilot, utilizing all of his resources to accomplish his ultimate goal. Although unaware of who may be on the other end of that call, he believes someone will be there to assist him. It is also because of his training that he knows he cannot wait until the last minute to make this distress call. In order for him to benefit from the assistance he has to make contact as soon as he realizes the situation is more than he can handle.

You should be the same way. God does not expect you to handle the storms of life by yourself. He has placed individuals in your life just for this purpose. The problem is we allow our circumstances or pride to hinder us from calling on them. Sometimes we do not realize they are there. The strength of others can be very beneficial when you can't see your own strength.

It would be great to develop a "main tower staff" before you get to a challenging point in life; however, we know it doesn't always work like that. The "main tower" is always there for you. God will provide every ounce of guidance and support. All you have to do is ask for it. He will also provide you with the wisdom to choose the people to help you in your time of need.

You don't need individuals who will just be sympathetic; you need individuals that are empathetic. Sympathy says "I feel bad for you," where empathy says "I have been in this situation myself, here is how I made it through," or, "I know it is hard, but you cannot stay here." You need individuals who will help you get to a point where you can stand on your own again. When you find yourself in a storm, it can be scary and even dangerous. Rest assured, you will get through this time and come out a better person in the process.

It was during a separation in my marriage that I realized the importance of making contact with the main tower and allowing His staff to guide me. I had reached rock bottom and could not see any sign of light. My marriage was everything to me and dealing with the separation had overcome me and taken complete control. All I wanted to do was lie in bed and cry. I went days without eating or showering. I got out of bed only long enough to take care of the needs of my children. Unaware of what I was going to do or how I was going to get out of this situation, I knew I had to do something. I did the only thing I could; I called out for help. I asked God for assistance. I had to seek help outside of myself because I had no strength and couldn't see past my circumstances. Although they did not know I was in need of help, my girlfriends reached out to me "just to see if I was okay." Looking back, I realize it was not a coincidence. I put in a distress call to the "main tower" and He instructed His people to help guide me through the storm. I thank God every day for my support group. These individuals had their hands full. There were times when the conversations were very brief and sometimes very lengthy. I can remember at one point the conversations were basically, "Get up and take a shower," or "Get up and eat." Had it not been for those instructions, I would have laid right there and possibly died in my storm.

The storms of life come when you become complacent and start to settle for less than what you desire. We have a tendency to place the needs of others before our own. I don't know if you caught what I said in the above paragraph: I was able to get out of bed long enough to take care of the needs of my children. Their well-being was more important than my own at that point. We devote so much time to what others need that we lose sight of what we need or desire. Other times it is just easier to focus on the needs of others because we do not have a clear picture of our own dreams or desires.

Understand, you deserve everything you desire. Never allow the dreams of other people to become so important that you disregard your own dreams. That is not how God designed the plan to work. If He gave you a dream, He has every intention for you to pursue it and achieve it. You may have individuals who will work against you. Those are the people that you need to steer away from. Understand everybody will not have your best interest at heart and that is okay. It is those people who have taught me to work harder. Know your true desires and push towards them.

School had always come easy for me. I loved learning. Throughout my school years, I had big dreams of what I wanted to do in life. It was my desire to work in the medical field. During high school, I excelled in all my health-related classes and was inspired by the advances that were being made in science. However, I felt something was missing. I was still struggling with my identity and desperately wanted to fit in with the popular clique. I began doing the things I saw them do in hopes that it would allow me the opportunity to become one of them. Although there were certain things I could never bring myself to do, like skipping class, I did participate in a few activities that could have easily caused me to get kicked out of school. It was against school policy to smoke on campus. But that didn't stop those who wanted to smoke. They simply went to the end of one of the buildings, quickly inhaled the cigarette and went back to class. Many times I was the lookout person, assuring that no one got caught. Soon I began to participate in this activity instead of just "being there." It wasn't my desire to smoke but soon it became a part of who I was. It helped me fit in with the crew and for once I felt like a member of the elite group. Now I realize I was lowering my standards in my desire to be a part of a group that probably would have never accepted me otherwise.

Although you have no control over how people act or the things they say, I do believe with everything I am, that people will treat you the way you allow them to treat you and how you treat yourself. If you don't demand to be loved, you won't be loved. If you don't desire that above average grade, you won't get it. If you do things just to fit into a group, they will always expect you to do what they do. If you don't pursue your dreams with everything you have, you won't achieve them. You can dream, you can set goals, but you will not be able to reach them by giving in to the first obstacle or hurdle that you encounter. Life is full of obstacles and hurdles. It is when you make up your mind to jump them that you will reap the blessings God has for you. There is nothing on this earth that is so important that it should distract you from your God-given dreams.

I felt my family was one of my God-given dreams and I was determined to make it work and continue building the masterpiece I called LIFE. My family was how I would feel love and how I could show love. I was willing to accept any form of love or affection that was given to me. It didn't matter how it was given as long as it felt like love. Soon I began to feel my desire to be loved or what I thought love was supposed to feel like was an illusion and seemingly unobtainable. Maybe the love I was searching for was just a figment of my imagination and really didn't exist. I had to learn how to be honest with myself. I didn't feel I deserved to be loved nor did I know what type of love I really desired. The only love I ever knew was the love of my parents, my grandmother, and the love I had for my child.

That was not the type of love I desired from my mate. I found myself trying to mold his love into the love that I had received before and giving him the same love that I had given to others. Needless to say that was not working. I pushed aside my support crew thinking that I no longer needed them. The reality of it all was I felt that if I kept them at bay, they would not be able to see the insurmountable pain that I was feeling. I was in a relationship that did not provide the support that I needed to grow. I was being verbally and mentally abused on a regular basis. I had isolated myself from all family and friends in order to prevent any type of conflict within my household. I put up walls and displayed a picture of harmony. I had an image to uphold. My entire life was consumed with my kids and my husband. There were times I felt so alone and depleted that all I could do was cry. It is a horrible thing to be alone when you are among people. The thing is, I didn't know why I was crying at the time. I now realize it was because I was full of discontentment and hopelessness; settling had become a part of my life.

I continually told myself "I had everything." I had a husband that gave me everything I desired (materialistically); I had well-mannered children; I had a big house that was immaculately taken care of because my job was to make sure it was clean. I can remember one day my husband came home from work and I had been cleaning all day. The entire house was cleaned, the children were bathed, and dinner was ready to be placed on the table. My husband stormed into the house and yelled, "Why is this dish towel on the table?" We can laugh at it now but at the time I was devastated. I immediately ran and removed the dish towel, looked at him and quickly stated, "You must have had a bad day at work. Go in the room and lie down for a while and unwind, I will bring your dinner to you." Walking through life on eggshells was a normal part of life; I was afraid to do anything wrong. I was afraid that I would do something to set him off and cause him to be upset. My job as his wife was to make his life peaceful. That was my purpose. I was willing to take all the ridicule and discontentment in order to provide my kids with the family I had always longed for. They seemed happy and that was all that mattered to me.

Being brought up in a single parent home and seeing my mother struggle to keep food on the table and a roof over our heads made me more determined to keep my family together by any means necessary. Even after it seemed that my marriage was over, I was determined to continue showing an image of togetherness. I was so emotionally drained. I was walking around like a zombie. My stoic attitude allowed me to hide the discontentment and helped me function on a daily basis. The feelings of confusion were no longer abnormal; they had become reality. My life seemed to always be in the spotlight. I had many people come up to me and comment on how great of a relationship we had and how well-behaved our children were. How could I let them down by telling them I wasn't happy and I was drowning in my own emotions? Yet I was screaming on the inside - I just wanted to be loved, to be accepted, and to be appreciated. What was I doing wrong? I felt I was giving everything I could to this relationship. I was providing a need even before it could be requested. I was making sure that everything was in place at all times. I felt I was in a constant screenplay and my life was the story line. I kept telling myself that any form of love was better than no love at all. I continued to tell myself that everything was okay; that I could do this, I could make this work. I learned to convince myself that what I had was good. Most of the women in our community worked outside of the house. My husband provided a lifestyle that allowed me to stay home and raise our children without financial concern. What I didn't realize was I was losing my own identity and killing my dreams.

There weren't many marriages in my past that modeled what a healthy relationship should look like. Many of the families in our community seemed to look fine from the outside but kids talk and I knew that many of them were dysfunctional and mediocre. I began to make excuses for feeling the way I was feeling. I was being selfish. How could I not be happy? Why didn't I feel love? I had more than some others. It had to be me. It had to be something I was doing wrong. I did not need much. I became consumed with not allowing my emotions to get the best of me. I began to put my feelings and desires on the back burner and soon forgot them altogether.

My desire to please was not just emotional. It was physical as well. My lack of self-esteem and the abuse began to take a toll on me physically. Although physical contact had never provided a sense of enjoyment for me, at this point in life it had become a mere task, something I did to satisfy my husband. As time progressed it became very difficult for me to focus on my own physical enjoyment because I wanted to assure that he was satisfied. Soon I began to tell myself that I didn't need it as long as he had what he desired. The truth of the matter is I did desire a physical connection even if only to be held, because some love was better than none. I began to associate sex with a form of love. Sex became my way of knowing that I existed in the family unit and sex was my way to connect with my husband. I began to see the material things that he provided as his way of showing love to the family. I began to rationalize every aspect of the situation. I felt that by blaming myself, I would be able to hold on to the hope that it could change. Of course that meant I would have to change. I had to find a way to make the situation better.

There set in the mode of complacency. I knew what I wanted, I knew what it was supposed to feel like, I knew how to give it but I didn't believe that I could have it or that I deserved it. When I began to dig into my issues, I realized I had been settling for a very long time. I learned that when you settle you are telling God that His desire for you to have life and have it more abundantly (John 10:10) is not enough for you. Abundantly means an overflow, to exceed the normal or the expected. When we look for man to provide that abundance of love that God speaks of, we are setting ourselves up to be let down every time. God's love is full of abundance. It supersedes all that we can think or ask. It will never fail. It will never run out. He does not require that we settle. He demands that we seek Him and He will give us what we need and desire. His Word declares that if we seek Him and Him alone we will never want for anything.

Allowing God to show His uncanny love for me allowed me to find the true unadulterated, unconditional love that I longed for. I no longer had to walk on eggshells or be afraid of not being enough or doing enough. I no longer had to use my physical contributions or the lack thereof to satisfy the needs of others. Most importantly, I began to love myself, realize that I am His child, and I deserve to have the best of the best. I learned that it was okay to receive love without being so consumed with the overwhelming concern of what the other person was expecting back. For the first time I was able to allow myself to be loved by my friends and family without the fear of letting them down. I was able to reach out to my support group and receive the love they were giving me without feeling like they wanted something in return. They were just showing me the love I had longed for.

Apply It

On a piece of paper write down the dreams you have for your life. Beside each one write down what you have settled for instead of pursuing the true dream you have. The idea here is not to look at what you wrote as a failure, but to identify where you are right now and make a commitment to move towards those dreams. You are deserving of those dreams and you are the only one who can make them happen. First you need to decide what it is you really desire. Consider each item you have written and ask yourself if it is something you can give yourself or does it require the help of another person. If it is something you can do for yourself, start doing it. If it requires the help of someone else, seek the help of your support group. They are there just for this purpose. If you don't have a support group, now is the time to seek God and develop one.

Dear God,
Help me to realize that I am deserving of my dreams. Help me to see that Your desire is for me to be happy and complete. Then help me to realize that You will place the individuals in my life who will help me accomplish every goal I desire to accomplish. Forgive me for not believing in Your plan and doing things my way. Help me to forgive myself for letting go of the desires You placed in my heart. Then help me to realize that it all begins with You. You will fulfill my dreams when I release them to You. Those things that I desire, those things that I crave, those things that seem impossible – help me realize You said all things are possible to them who believe. I have settled and it has caused discontentment in my life. I thank You in advance for replacing it with harmony and hope. Where I have placed a lower standard of love and acceptance in my life I ask You to help me accept You as my source of love and acceptance. In Jesus' Name I pray.

My Secret Lover

> *"The courage to be is the courage to accept oneself, in spite of being unacceptable."* ~Paul Tillich
>
> *"Your problem is you're... too busy holding onto your unworthiness."* ~Ram Dass

No one is exempt from becoming addicted to something. There are many definitions for the word addiction but for this purpose we will use the following definitions: an uncontrollable compulsion to repeat a behavior regardless of its negative consequences; a compulsive dependence on a behavior or substance. Many feel an addict is a person addicted to a controlled substance or "drug". But when there is a lack for something you truly desire, anything can become a "drug."

When you begin to look for alternatives to cover up the way you feel, the things you desire, or who you really are inside and you begin to replace those things repeatedly with complete and total disregard as to the consequences or effect it is having on your person and those around you, you are addicted. Addictions come in all shapes and forms.

Society has begun to downplay any addiction that is not an illegal substance. There are many people who are addicted to exercise, attention, work, control, and even religion. We begin to replace that desire to be loved and appreciated with whatever is made available and can soon make it a part of a secret love affair. Many drug addicts associate their drug of choice with a lover. Nothing else matters, all they can think of is that next fix. There are people who live just for the next adrenaline rush from their drug of choice.

During my late teens and early twenties, I was looking to be loved and accepted and I began to cover my pain by eating. I found that food was the only thing that did not judge me, turn me down or make me feel like a failure. This was the only thing that I was truly doing for myself - eating. I can remember feeling as though at times I was just throwing things in my mouth, not because I was hungry but because I was hurting, I was lonely, and food comforted me. It didn't matter what it was; it could be candy, chips, a salad – it really didn't matter as long as it was something. One day I woke up and realized I was almost 350 pounds and addicted to food. I wanted to crawl under a bus and die. How? Why did I do this to myself?

My eating was a direct hit to myself. I felt that if I was going to be treated like nothing, looking the part was the only thing left to do. There was that negative consequence to my actions. I was sure no one loved me, no one understood me, and no one wanted me. I saw food as my "everything." It was my friend, it was my lover, and it was my confidant. It never judged me, it never mistreated me or so I thought.

I found myself hiding what I was eating even hiding where I was eating. When I was sad – I ate. When I was lonely – I ate. When I was bored – I ate. As I ate, the weight piled on and I found myself trapped inside a thick shell. I felt it was a physical boundary that I had set for myself. This was something I could do for myself that no one else could control or take away. I was determined to be in control of something in my life. It was working. Nothing could come in and hurt me, it was my shield. What I soon realized was that nothing was coming in but nothing was going out either.

I soon got to the point where I was completely confused and lost. I didn't know who I was anymore or what my true purpose in life was. I was walking around in total disbelief of my surroundings and had completely lost control of my life. The one thing I thought I was in control of was actually controlling me. Walking up the stairs became an insurmountable task. The more I wanted to be accepted and loved, the more set apart I felt. Regardless of what I did I began to feel my weight was a cause of more failure.

I began to blame my weight for the causes of all the turmoil in my life. I became consumed by the weight. Each day brought back all the memories associated with the name calling and insults that I endured when I was a kid. When I went up in the tree to play with my doll, it wasn't completely to be "prissy," it was because I was tired and couldn't keep up with the boys anymore. Even then, in my doll bag was treats. Allowing honesty to seep in, I was courting my secret lover back then. One of the things that I remember most about visits with my father prior to his death was going to my tree, laughing, talking, and eating a candy bar, a pickled pig foot and drinking a cola. Every time he came to visit me that was something I could expect – it was our "time" together. In fact, everyone catered to that side of me. I always had some kind of treat waiting for me.

When I was around 14, I went to babysit my cousin in New Jersey. This was the first time I had been away from my family since my father's death when I was nine years old. That summer I fell in love or should I say a deep "like". There was this boy who told me I was cute and that my curves made me stand out from the other girls there. Then he said what I longed to hear. He said he liked me. This was the first time since my father's death that someone had shown me attention like that. Every day we would walk up and down the streets talking and laughing and enjoying each other's company. When I returned home, family and friends were in awe. They couldn't believe how much weight I had lost. They began to treat me differently – they wanted to be around me and talk to me. It was then that fear and insecurity took control and again, I felt out of place. Where was all this attention coming from? Just a few months before it seemed as if I couldn't find anyone to give me attention and now it was all around me. At first I enjoyed all the attention; for the first time I was accepted. Then as quick as all the attention began, it slowly disappeared again. Not because people changed but because I changed, and what I was getting just wasn't enough. It was a rush and I wanted more. However, that attention comes with a price.

Once I entered into high school things began to change. Because I had never learned to associate or connect with females, many of my associates at that time were males. The girls began to shun and belittle me. I am not sure if it was because they were intimidated by the relationship I had with the guys or if they just saw me as a threat. There was never a physical connection between me and the guys. I could just relate to them. Then something changed. The boys began to take on different characteristics. They became interesting and cute. I was starting to like the attention they gave me as they commented on my curves and the way I acted around them. I began to crave that attention. Their words began to validate me and it felt good.

Soon I realized, I was a part of the group – a real part. They seemed to want to be around me. My addiction shifted from food to attention. Oh how I craved the attention. If someone didn't comment on how I looked, it brought my spirits down. If they did, I was excited, but soon the guys were no longer just commenting on how I looked but they wanted to touch and hug on me. I just liked being told I was cute; touching was not a part of the plan, I was not ready for that. Although it seemed I was now a part of this wonderful group, I was still very insecure. Those insecurities made me feel that the attention was a part of a hidden agenda. If someone is paying this much attention to me they must want something from me. I began to shy away from all the attention and I found myself knocking on the doors of seclusion again.

I struggled continuously with my weight through much of my life. It seemed the only time I was in control of my weight was when I was being validated by another person- usually a guy. My emotions were all over the place. I liked the attention and the compliments I received but I didn't like the feelings that came with those compliments. I just wasn't used to having someone like me. The validation of one particular young man sparked something in me that allowed me to desire the touch that I had been pushing away for so long. During this courtship I became pregnant and gained a lot of weight. I was still in high school. Once that happened, there were no more compliments about my curves and the attention from the other guys stopped. What happened? I was still the same person.

When I finally decided enough was enough and I was going to do something about the "baby" weight, several things happened. At first I was excited about losing the weight and began to like what I saw. But then the attention both negative and positive that I received as the pounds dropped off became more than I could bear. I was unable to decipher whether people were genuinely proud of me or if they were being sarcastic because I still saw myself as the fat person. The weight was heavier off than it was on. I thought that by losing the weight I would be happy again. The compliments would return. Life would be better. Unfortunately losing the weight did not change anything, I was still miserable. I still felt out of place and disconnected. It still felt like I had a yoke upon my neck.

I became obsessed with the weight. I weighed myself every day. If I was up a pound, I wouldn't eat. If I was down a pound, I felt I could eat. The problem wasn't what I was eating, it was what was eating me. I was not happy. I was lost. I was hurting. Once again I found myself wanting, desiring, and struggling to fit in, to be accepted. I felt that every bad thing that happened somehow had to be associated with me and my weight.

The year after my baby was born, his father left for college. The overwhelming feeling of being a single parent was stifling. My mother encouraged me to go out with my friends, but I did not feel like I fit into that group anymore. I was the only one who had a child and I was once again struggling with my identity and insecurities.

I grew tired of the isolation and made a decision to venture out, to have some fun. A friend of a friend told me about this party and suggested that I go. Excited that I had been invited to a party, I jumped at the opportunity. My mom had agreed to watch the baby and I was off to have some fun. Once I arrived at the location, my intuition told me something was not right. I pushed those feelings aside, thinking it was just my paranoia taking over. I needed to have some fun. I walked up to the door, knocked and the guy opened the door. I did not hear any music nor did I see anyone. He informed me that I was early and that he was setting up. Naïve and accepting, I walked into the worst moment of my life. After entering the room, the man began to physically assault me. He slapped me. He punched me. He threatened me. He violated me. When he was finished, he told me if I told anyone what happened he would kill me. Feeling completely helpless and ashamed, I drove home in shock. I don't even remember driving home. The assault played over and over in my head the entire trip. What just happened? Why would someone want to do this to me? Who can I tell?

I went home and washed for what seemed like hours, then I grabbed my baby and cried myself to sleep. I sat in my room, in the dark for the next few days. I put a blanket up to the windows during the day to make it dark, telling my mother that I had a headache and the light hurt my eyes. I was so ashamed. I did not go anywhere. I did not do anything other than hold my baby, eat, and cry. I thought everyone would be able to see through my pain and begin to ask questions. I didn't even allow my mother to get close to me during that time. As I sat in that room I was repulsed by my own image. I replayed the entire scene over and over in my head. As I cried, I ate. I was trying to mask the feelings of disgust and hatred. How could I allow something like this to happen? What made me think someone liked me enough to want me to come to an actual party? How was I going to tell the father of my child what happened? Who was I going to tell? Would this guy really kill me if I told anyone? As the questions formed, I ate. I ate so much one day that I became violently sick. Yet after being sick, I ate some more. I just wanted to disappear. I wanted to escape the thoughts in my head. I had been in my room now for four days. My mom began to get concerned, threatening to take me to the doctor. All she knew was I was throwing up and had a migraine. She didn't know that at this point I was making myself throw up trying to replace the pain of the event and eating way too much. To avoid any further confrontations, I began to make myself seen throughout the house, but I would not leave. The house was my safe haven.

My boyfriend, my baby's father, had been calling and could tell something was not right. He began to interrogate me over and over, insisting that something was wrong. He could hear it in my voice. Unsatisfied with my answer, the following weekend he came home. I told him what had happened. All the pain associated with that night came back as he scolded and blamed me for what happened. All the shame and disgust I felt those four days came back as I watched him drive off. I went in the house and began medicating myself with my routine of eating and throwing up. After what seemed like weeks, my throat was raw, my stomach was in knots and I was in complete pain. My mother insisted that I go to the doctor. It seemed that once I left the house, reality hit and I realized I had to do something. The physical and mental pain was more than I could take. I began to cry out, "God make it stop!!"

When I returned home from the doctor's office, I sat down and told my grandmother what happened. She insisted that I talk to a rape counselor. It was the best decision I could have made. She helped me realize that what happened was not my fault and that I could not blame myself for the choices of other people. The sessions helped me to forgive myself and the young man for events that happened over that two week period. I realized it was my desire to be accepted that kept me from exposing that happened. I did not want anyone to be upset with me. I blamed myself and felt everyone else would too.

Whether it was an addiction to food or an addiction to attention, I was lost and out of control. I wish I could say the counseling sessions cured my addiction to food. I continued to have this secret affair for many years. I was fighting for attention and I was using whatever I could to get it. I still battle with food addiction. I've just learned how to keep it under control. Yes, there are times when I am eating and I'm not hungry. Yes, there are times that I turn to junk food when what I really want is attention.

I have my ups and downs and you will too. Please don't think that once you identify your addiction it will disappear. That's when it becomes the hardest to control. Remember the enemy, whether it is a spiritual attack or an attack of your own mind, can only use the weapons we give him. It wasn't until I realized that my battle with food was associated with my insecurities, that I became more aware of my insecurities and my desire to fit in. I began to make up stories in my head. I began to feel that I just wasn't good enough. Then God stepped in and reminded me that I was His child and that I was more than enough.

Once I accepted the love He has for me, the lies in my head slowed down and the battles became less. I learned when I was feeling unloved or needed attention, to call out to God. I learned to love myself, to treat myself the way I want others to treat me, with the love and respect that I gave them. The most important thing I learned is that no one would or could love me more than God. I am a wonderfully created vessel of God. We all have our struggles and addictions, but you must look deep inside and find what it is you are really searching for, what it is that you really need. Until then, that thing you try to fill the emptiness with will never be enough.

Apply It

Ask yourself what are you hiding behind? What is your drug of choice? What have you tried to control only to find it has controlled you? Now realize you are not alone. There are many people struggling with insecurities and inadequacies every day. Stop beating yourself up and allowing the negative thoughts in your head to control your outward thinking. The only way to combat those thoughts is to make a conscious decision to do so. Now write a letter of forgiveness to yourself. This letter is to be an apology for all the negative things you have said to yourself, all the times you have felt unacceptable, undesirable, and unloved by the only one who matters – YOU! You are a child of the Most High King and He loves you more than anything. He desires for you to live life free of insecurities. You can do this.

Dear God,
Help me to forgive all the negative things I have said to myself. Help me to accept myself as You created me. Help me to remember that You love me regardless of how I look. You love me for who I am. Then God help me to love myself as You love me, accept myself as You accept me. Teach me to surrender my all to You and watch as You work in my life. In Jesus' Name I pray.

But My Vows

"This day I will marry my friend, the one I laugh with, live for, dream with, love." ~ Unknown

"Most marriages can survive 'better or worse.' The tester is all the years of 'exactly the same.'" ~Robert Brault

Marriage is sacred. It is designed to unite two people as one. It is a bond that is not easily broken if you allow God to be the glue that holds it together. Trials and tribulations are inevitable. When I spoke with couples who have been married for a couple of years or those married for thirty years or more, all have identified that there have been struggles. No one I have come into contact with has ever said it was easy. No one will testify that it does not require work. What I learned through personal experience and from those whom I've had a chance to talk with concerning marriage, after the trust is broken, it is hard to repair without God working in the midst.

Trust and respect go hand in hand. Trust is defined as having an extreme confidence in something or someone. Respect is defined as having a highly positive esteem for something or someone. Once you've lost trust in a person, the respect for that person will soon follow and vice versa. It is hard to respect someone that you cannot trust. It is even harder to trust someone you cannot respect. Once a marriage has encountered this type of loss, only God can make the necessary repairs, and even when He steps in, it requires work on both behalves to repair what was broken.

In today's society, infidelity has become common. It seems rare to find a marriage that has not encountered at least one battle with infidelity. My marriage was no exception to the rule. Infidelity struck and ripped away every ounce of self-worth that I had built over the years. It left me feeling like a complete failure. I questioned everything about myself, everything about my husband, and everything about our marriage. My marriage was a major part of my identity. It signified my purpose. It signified my position. In my mind, it signified ME.

I knew my marriage was in grave danger and I fought to hold on. The only thing I had to hold on to was my vows. There were times I questioned them, but I continued to hold on. I continued to fight. My family was everything to me. If it ended, what would that say about me? What would I do if I wasn't married? What would God say? I was taught that you should not divorce. I was taught that if you make a vow you should keep it. All my life I told myself I would not be like so many others in my family that allowed their marriages to end in divorce. I would break that generational curse. Here I stood looking at what could be the end of my marriage and had no way of fixing it. The words I repeated during my wedding ceremony played loudly in my ears. They played like a bass drum beating in an offbeat. It was nagging. It was overwhelming. It was deafening. Yet I couldn't figure out what to do about it.

As I questioned my vows, many questions arose in my mind. What did they really mean? What had I really committed to? I began to analyze each portion of my vows, trying to find something that would give me permission not to feel so obligated. But there was nothing there. What I was forced to do, was to see my vows for what they really were.

Let me break them down the way I saw them:
"We are gathered here today before God and before family and friends to join this man and woman..." To me that said: "You made this commitment before God and all your friends and family; now make it work or you will be seen as a liar and a failure."

All the words concerning marriage being honorable among men and not entering into it unadvisedly or lightly –I was living in sin and needed to get married so I would be found honorable before God. Who am I kidding? I wanted to be honorable before man – I was pregnant and didn't want to have another baby out of wedlock. I wanted to be married. That would signify that I was accepted and loved.

When I recited the actual vows, I meant every word. I knew what I was saying, I knew what I wanted and I knew that I would forever keep my promise. I would love him, cherish him, I would comfort him, I would keep him – I would forsake all others and cling to him. (I did that part well).

Now I know that isn't exactly how the vows go and I did that deliberately: "in sickness and in health, for richer, for poorer, for better, for worse, in sadness and in joy…as long as we both shall live." Yes – I will! We both recited them – I feel at the time we both meant them. I feel we just didn't know what we were saying and what it really meant. But I knew that I had made a vow and I was not going to go back on it. My vow was to God as well as to my husband.

I think vows should specifically say "I will not abuse, I will not cheat, I will not hurt" – and then people would be more careful of what they are saying to each other.

As I began to examine my vows, there were still portions that haunted me. The "for better or worse" statement confused me. Was an affair a part of the better or worse? Was physical and verbal abuse a part of the better or worse? Some may say yes – but through prayer I began to realize anything that destroys who you are physically and/or spiritually is not what God would have for you to be attached to. I was then released from the psychological hold my vows had on me. I was able to understand that my vows did not require that I stay in an abusive relationship. They did not require that I stay in a situation that did not allow me to fulfill the purpose that God had given me. I realized God would not desire me to be in any relationship that would become more important than Him.

There were two other parts in those vows that I can honestly say when we broke them, began the ultimate demise of our marriage: keep God first and always remain each other's best friend. At the beginning, God was not first in our marriage. We eventually developed a relationship with God and attended church on a regular basis. Soon we began to teach Bible study classes and move deeper into ministry. As time went on, we began to learn all the Christian lingo and how to put on a front for the people during those times when our relationship was not on the best of terms. There were days we would ride to church and not say anything to each other, go into the church like everything was grand, ride back home in silence, and go into separate corners once we entered the house. We had even mastered putting on a front for our children. We made it all look so loving. Soon the charade became more than either of us could bear and our friendship began to suffer. We began to seek other people to share our concerns with. Eventually all communication became obsolete.

The other part of my vows I struggled with was: "what God has joined together let no man put asunder." The definition I choose to use for asunder is - to be apart from each other either in position or direction. Let me clarify, I believe that God had ordained my marriage. He allowed it to produce some awesome miracles. My children are the result of this wonderful marriage. The hundreds of souls that were ministered to on a weekly basis through speaking of things we learned throughout our marriage were all a part of our walk together as a couple. There were many couples we were able to counsel because of our union. Yes, God brought us together for a specific purpose. The problem was we began to put all of those things before our own relationship. We stopped doing anything together and enjoying each other's company. We put ourselves asunder. We began to grow in different directions and took a different position on our views. We forgot our joint vision. We forgot our purpose. We forgot our vows to each other.

When the infidelity began, we were not in a position to discuss our concerns or challenges. We both became consumed with our own objectives. The only thing we came together to discuss was the children and church. I'm not giving excuses for the infidelity, but I am addressing the issues that allowed it to happen.

The distance in my marriage brought back all the insecurities I had faced growing up. I couldn't understand what I was doing that would cause him to mistreat me and ultimately cheat on me. I began to pour myself into the Bible in hopes that it would help me to understand. For a while, it seemed to help and on the surface my spiritual life was growing but my physical situation became more than I could handle. I became depressed and did not want to live. I remember asking God to take me out of my misery. Thankfully He ignored my request.

When your relationship with man begins to be more important than your relationship with God, it is time to examine that relationship. God is a jealous God and He does not want anyone or anything put before Him. The Bible is clear in stating that we should have no other gods before Him. (Exodus 20:3). It took the demise of my marriage for me to develop a true authentic relationship with God. I do not want that for you. I want you to understand that God loves you and wants to fill your every desire; even relationships with other people. But before you can love anyone, you have to love yourself. That was my mistake. I did not learn to love to myself prior to making those vows. It was not until God came in and showed me true love that I was able to love someone else.

Apply It

What have you been taught through society or family that keeps you from living a life that God has called for you to live? What are you putting before God? Write those things on a piece of paper. Look at them and decide if they are commands from God or commands from man. Your first vow is to GOD. Anything on your list that would interrupt your God-given purpose must be removed. It may be hard but God will help you if you ask Him.

Dear God,

Help me to honor my vow to You. Help me to be what You have called me to be. Help me to realize that You are a jealous God and You will have no one placed before You. Help me to realize that when I place someone before You I am going against Your commandments and against my vow to You. Help me to walk in the path that You have designed for me and not the path that I want to walk down. In Jesus' Name I pray.

The Dream

> "Watch a man in times of... adversity to discover what kind of man he is; for then at last words of truth are drawn from the depths of his heart, and the mask is torn off." ~Lucretius, On the Nature of Things

> "If you must love your neighbor as yourself, it is at least as fair to love yourself as your neighbor." ~Nicholas de Chamfort

I once had a dream that began with me standing on a stage, full of excitement. There were thousands of people from all over and from all walks of life. It was a massive audience; I couldn't see where the crowd ended. They were there to hear a word from God. My husband had been chosen to minister and I was given the honor of introducing him. I was so excited and so proud of the accomplishments he had made. The image was breath-taking and I was on top of the world. I began my introduction by telling the crowd how important it was to always put your best efforts forth, to have a dream and to pursue your true calling. As I was talking everyone began to laugh and point at me and I couldn't figure out why. The excitement of speaking to the crowd began to vanish. Why were they laughing? What I was saying wasn't funny, this was a serious moment. I looked around to see what they could be laughing at. Then I looked down and realized I was completely naked; I had on nothing. I began to try to cover my body. I began to cry. I was so embarrassed. I looked around to see where I could run and realized there was nowhere to go. I then noticed my husband standing at the end of the stage holding a blanket. I knew he would come to my rescue. This was my husband, my partner, my life. As I looked at him, I noticed that he was laughing with everyone else. He had no intention of bringing the blanket to me, of covering me, of protecting me, of shielding me. He was laughing just as hard if not harder than everyone else. Why is he laughing at me? Isn't he supposed to be the one to protect me in a situation like this? I ran towards him and tried to grab the blanket but he wouldn't let go of it. I was devastated.

I woke up with tears rolling down my face. My heart was beating fast. I was shaking from fear. It all seemed so real. Was this a dream or was it reality? As I looked over at the man lying beside me, thinking how he had just abandoned me in my dream, I could not determine if I was angry or hurt. It had not been many years ago that he had vowed to protect me and to take care of me through it all. Yet here I lay feeling abandoned and alone.

I soon determined this dream was a reality check. It was an opportunity for me to see a scene in my life that I otherwise would have never been able to identify. This dream was actually my reality. I had focused all my attention on pushing the accomplishments of others and helping them to achieve their dreams.

This dream taught me so much about myself. I was weak, I was vulnerable, I didn't know how to love myself therefore I couldn't really love others or allow others to love me. I depended on someone else to protect me. I could stand before a crowd in complete belief and support of someone else but had no belief in myself. I was lost. I was lonely. I was miserable. It was that moment standing on stage completely naked, having such strong feelings take over my mind and body when I realized I didn't know who I was or what I wanted out of life. I made a promise to myself that I would fix that. Never again would I feel that incomplete, that unloved, that unfinished.

I made a conscious decision to take time to figure out what I wanted out of life. What would make me happy? What could I do for myself that would push me towards fulfilling my own dreams? I sat down and wrote out my dreams, all the things that I had given up on, the things I felt I could never accomplish, even things that others told me I would never accomplish. Then I began to make smaller goals, things that would help me to see some accomplishment towards the bigger picture. As I began to accomplish those goals, my attitude about myself began to change. I began to feel that I deserved to have dreams. I began to feel that my dreams were worthy of pursuing. Soon I saw a light within myself and I liked it.

As I worked through some major issues, the dream re-occurred. This time it was a little different. I was still standing on stage before a massive group, talking about pursuing your true calling and the laughter began. I looked down and realized I was naked. I was able to put a smile on my face. Another difference I noticed was this time I did not run off stage embarrassed – I reached down and covered certain areas and told the crowd – "some things don't need to be shared with the whole world". I walked over and took the blanket from my husband, wrapped it around myself, walked back to the podium and continued my speech. It was at that time I received a standing ovation. People realized that I was secure in myself and my abilities and they were willing to help me celebrate it. Another thing that I observed was I was there to present to that crowd. It was me that they had come to hear.

I can remember the first time I was asked to speak before a group, I was actually terrified. I did not want to let the people down nor did I want my presentation to be misunderstood. I had to reach deep down inside myself and ask for help. It was at that time I made a decision that I would pursue my dreams. I would use my story to motivate and encourage others.

Sometimes it takes situations that make you feel uncomfortable or even abandoned to force you to pursue your true calling. Each one of us has been given a job to accomplish while we are here on Earth. After being forced out of my comfort zone, I was able to identify what my true dream consisted of. I wanted to encourage people. I wanted to use my testimony to help women who struggled with low self-esteem and those who had been mistreated by the people they loved.

Apply It

What are your dreams? Have you pushed them aside because you felt you were not capable of accomplishing them? What have you been told you could never do? Those are the things that God wants to use to help others. Remember if you were able to accomplish them by yourself, you would not need help from God. He's there waiting for you to ask for His help and for you to walk into your true calling. Write those dreams down on a piece of paper. Now write down three things you can accomplish within the next three weeks that can lead you towards those goals.

Dear God,

Thank You for allowing things that seem unbearable to enter into my life. Now help me to see those things as an opportunity to do better and to believe in myself. I realize that I am nothing without You but that with You, I can do all things. Help me to remember when it seems that the world has turned its back on me, You are always right there to provide cover, protection and direction. In Jesus' Name I pray.

Will the Real You Stand up?

> *"The doorstep to the temple of wisdom is knowledge of our own ignorance."* - Benjamin Franklin
>
> *"The man who has no inner life is a slave to his surroundings."* ~Henri Frédéric Amiel

As a little girl, I had this dream that I would be swept off my feet and fall in love and build a life that would be the talk of the town. For a while it was. I had the type of life that people dreamed of being part of. I was married to my best friend, I had great kids who excelled in school, my house was a home and everyone knew they were welcome, my husband had a promising and vibrant ministry and I was doing everything I could to live up to the virtuous woman parable. I felt my dear husband would forever be there for me and the kids, that he would always protect me and love me. I wanted to be everything I could be for him. I wanted him to be happy, and I wanted him to love me unconditionally and never be sad because of anything I did. As I saw it, everything was perfect, I had the best of everything or so I thought. But now looking back I realize I was living someone else's life, a life that others wanted for me.

I remember saying to myself, "I'm happy when others around me are happy." The sad thing about that is I believed it. It wasn't until I started working through the issues of my life that I realized that was NOT true. I also realized I didn't know what happy felt like so how could I share it with others?

Yet I put up a good front. I had everyone convinced that everything was great, that my life was perfect and all was well. Sadly I had myself believing it too. I kept telling myself that this is the way it was supposed to be. This was my sacrifice for having the abundance that God had promised me. I wasn't in pain, this was normal. I just needed to push through, put on a thicker skin and watch for my blessings at the end. Keep the main thing the focus. Nothing else really mattered. As a mother, as a wife, my life was centered on the needs of my family. I didn't have needs anymore. I was walking around with a painted-on smile and inside I was dying, literally.

I needed the "real me" to stand up. I needed to find a way for that little girl inside of me to stop feeling the need to fade into the background. When I began to work on finding that person and fighting for that little girl, I was told I was being selfish and self-centered. That was not what I wanted to display so I retreated back into my little hole. I didn't want to displease anyone. I wanted to be accepted, to be loved- so if I was being selfish, that was bad. I later realized that it was not selfishness, it was self-care. Self- care is loving yourself and providing support for yourself so you can achieve your goals. I was taking the time to care for me, the way no one else could. I had to look deep inside and find out what I needed in life – what I wanted in life.

I can remember so many times feeling guilty for doing simple things for myself. Purchasing a pair of earrings made me feel as if I had in some way neglected the needs of my family by spending a couple dollars on myself. I can remember going to the gym and feeling as if I was a bad person because surely my kids needed me to help them do something –I had to make sure they sat far enough away from the television so that it didn't ruin their eyes or something. I had to be there just in case. Soon I realized that not taking care of me was hindering them from being who they were called to be. I was teaching them that they didn't deserve to be loved or cared for not even by themselves. I was teaching them that I was afraid to stand up for myself and express how I felt. I was also teaching them and others how to treat me. I didn't care enough about myself to take the time to care for myself. God had trusted me to care for these lives and I was not upholding my end of the deal. It was then that I decided the real me needed to stand up. I began to set goals for myself and make every effort to make them come to pass. I began to tell myself that I was good enough and that I deserved to be treated well. I began to treat myself the way I wanted others to treat me. I began to stop allowing others to speak negativity into my life and more importantly I stopped speaking negativity into my life. I was standing up!

Every day was not successful. I fell back into bad habits on more than one occasion. But I learned how to identify those habits and worked towards making them few and far between. It was hard for me to stand up for myself, so I elected to fight for the little girl who was crying on the inside of me.

Some may think it was a bit psychotic to advocate for a part of yourself. But for me, it was therapeutic. I've always been an advocate for others, but I never had the courage to fight for myself. When I identified a part of me that had been crying out for love and attention all my life, my heart reached for her.

I began small by imagining I was purchasing her a pair of earrings or I was taking her to the gym to play with her friends. I began to not allow individuals to speak any kind of way in her presence. I began to change the environment in which she dwelled. I began to dress differently. I began to take care of myself inwardly and outwardly. The result of taking care of this little person made a major impact on me. I began to walk by the mirror and admire what I saw looking back at me. I began to feel that I was somebody and I deserved to be treated as such.

Now you may not need to be as dramatic as I was but you do need to allow the real you to stand up and advocate for your space in your own life. It is not a matter of being selfish or self-centered. It is merely taking the time to provide self-care for the most important person in your life. We hear so many times, "you cannot love others until you learn to love yourself." I really did not believe that until I began to nurture the little girl who was crying out to be loved.

There was a young lady who worked with me who seemed very sad and lonely. As she walked up and down the hallways, she never looked up or made eye contact with anyone. One day I approached her and we began a very intense dialogue. After talking with her I found out this young lady was very depressed but had learned to mask her feelings by detaching herself from her surroundings. That night I went home and re-examined my own situation. I realized that I, too, had learned how to mask my emotions by detaching myself and focusing on others. Having that mirrored image displayed before me was a complete eye opener. I was able to see what I looked like to others. I always thought I was portraying a happy and approachable person, when in actuality I was very stand-offish and isolated.

That idea of how I presented myself haunted me. That was not how I wanted to be received. I began to make a deliberate effort to smile and make eye contact with people as I approached them. I did not realize how hard it was to smile. I did not realize the effort it took to make eye contact. What I did realize was that by doing these simple things, it made me more approachable. I began to laugh more. I began to talk to people in a more friendly way. I began to want to be around people and they wanted to be around me. I enjoyed my own company. I was no longer focused on all the bad things that had happened in my life. I was focused on the things that made me happy.

I remember sitting in my living room laughing with my children. My daughter stopped mid-laughter and gave me this very strange look. Perplexed by her look, I asked her what was wrong. She informed me that it was the first time she had ever heard me laugh and I was radiating with joy. At first the statement hurt me but then I embraced it and began to accept that I was changing and allowing the real me to stand up.

You never have to be ashamed of who you are. Anyone who makes you feel uncomfortable in their presence is not someone you should be devoting that much energy to. I went through a period where I had to disconnect myself from individuals who tried to intimidate me and smother my ability to love myself. At first I thought I was being mean. I was even told by some of these individuals that my actions were ungodly. I realize now that making the decision to place boundaries was the best thing I could have done for my own growth.

Realize that just because you disconnect with individuals for a period of time, does not mean you can never invite them back into your circle. It does give you an opportunity to be true to yourself and the ability to love yourself enough to make a conscious decision about whether those individuals deserve a place in your circle. You are a special individual who deserves to be treated as such. As I stated earlier, I was teaching people how to treat me by the way I allowed them to treat me and the way I treated myself. Once I began to treat myself with respect and demand respect from individuals in my circle, I began to receive the love and respect that I so desperately desired. In return, it made me a happier person who people desired to be around.

Apply It

Make a point of doing something just for you every day for the next ten days. It can be something small. It does not have to require finances. You can take a walk around the park. You can give yourself a manicure. You can take a hot bath. You can even treat yourself to a movie. Each night before you go to bed write down what the event was and how it made you feel. Did you find yourself uneasy or uncomfortable? Was it difficult? If you answered yes, explain why. My prayer is that you will eventually realize that you deserve to be treated well.

Dear God,

Help me to take care of myself. Help me to realize that taking care of myself does not make me selfish, it helps show others how I desire to be cared for and it helps me learn to respect when others care for themselves. Father help me to see that You have great expectations for me and that if I don't allow the real me to step forward I am not living the life you would have for me to live. In Jesus' Name I pray, Amen.

Life Begins Now

"Don't be discouraged. It's often the last key in the bunch that opens the lock." ~Author Unknown

"I may not be there yet, but I'm closer than I was yesterday." ~Author Unknown

A wise man once told me that "when you're in your twenties, you find yourself doing everything you are big and bad enough to do. When you're in your thirties, you are looking for ways to repair all the damage you did during your twenties and it's not until you turn forty and look back at what you have accomplished and the trials and tribulations that you have triumphed through that you really begin to enjoy life." I have to say that was the best advice I have ever received. It helped me to accept where I am and what I have been through. It also helped me to realize that changing any of the experiences in my life would change the person I am today. The experiences from my late teens and early twenties structured my character and taught me to persevere. The struggles experienced in my thirties gave me wisdom and strength and taught me to depend on God.

People may ask why I would embrace the emotions and heartache associated with my past, including the pain of losing my father at an early age and feeling abandoned, the pain of seeing my mother physically and emotionally abused in relationships, the hurt from the kids in the neighborhood bullying me and calling me names, and the scars experienced from the emotional and physical abuse in my own relationship. I realize that each one of those experiences have equipped me for my God-given purpose. I understand my purpose is to encourage individuals who have experienced similar situations and help them move forward without judgment.

There are several vivid moments that are burnt into my memory but I can remember one in particular. Times were extremely hard and I had prepared dinner for my children. I realized there would be just enough food for them, so I prepared their plates, called them to the dinner table, prayed with them and went outside on the deck while they ate. Although I went to bed hungry that night, I was satisfied in knowing that I did the best I could to meet the needs of my children and provide for them.

Memories from your past do not have to torment you. You should use them as a measurement of how far you have come. Every obstacle in your life should bring an opportunity to grow your belief and faith in God.

No one desires to go through pain. If I could have gone through life without experiencing pain, that would have been great. But these life experiences have taught me to be strong. They have taught me how to weather the storms of life. They have taught me how to love. They have taught me to continue on. It is those moments that keep me humble. It was those moments and those moments alone that will help me to be compassionate when someone comes to me hungry or in pain.

It will be those moments that will help me to understand how someone can stay in an abusive relationship or allow someone to mistreat or neglect them. It is those moments that will help me to remember what it's like not to love yourself. Most importantly it is those moments that will help me to be grateful for my deliverance. It is those moments that God will use to heal someone else.

Life is full of teachable moments. It just requires that you take those moments that you are afforded and apply them. Many times we sit and complain about what we don't have but it's when you learn to appreciate what you do have that you will receive more. God has an abundance waiting for you and He has a great desire to give it to you, but you will never be able to receive more until you learn to be grateful for what you already have. Circumstances may be hard for you right now. You may not even know what your next step will be but understand you are a child of God and He loves you unconditionally. Nothing in life is coincidental. Everything happens for a reason. God has not forgotten you. He loves you. Take your eyes off your problems and put them on God.

Apply It

Take a brief moment and think about a situation in life when you felt you would never be able to overcome. It may even be your current situation. It could be something that happened years ago. Regardless of what it is, realize there was a lesson in it for you. Now think of what that lesson was and how you have grown from it. The thought may be painful but I need you to focus on and embrace your victory. Write about that experience in your journal.

Dear God,
You have given me so many opportunities to learn from life. Instead of focusing on the lessons, I chose to focus on the pain. Father, I ask You to forgive me and help me learn to use what You have given me as a testimony of Your grace and mercy. Help me to move through my pain and use it to help and encourage others. In Jesus' Name I pray.

You can Lead a Horse to Water

> *"Respect your efforts, respect yourself. Self-respect leads to self-discipline. When you have both firmly under your belt, that's real power."*
> ~Clint Eastwood

> *"If you don't like something change it; if you can't change it, change the way you think about it."* ~Mary Engelbreit

For many years I lived my life walking in someone else's shoes and acting like they fit. I wanted to be the best daughter in order to make my mom the best mother. If I could just do the right thing, get the best grades, and keep my room clean, she would not have to be so stressed and she would be able to spend the time with me that I craved. If I would give in to my children's request just this time and say yes to the things that I knew were not good for them, I would be deemed the best mother in the world and they would love me unconditionally. If I would say yes to all the demands requested by family and friends then they would all be happy and I would be accepted. If I would love my husband just a little more, prepare his favorite meals, make his life just a little bit easier, I would be deemed the best wife and receive the love I desired from him. I was trying to identify the needs of others in order to satisfy my own needs. What a big price to pay just to walk in some shoes that didn't fit. The sad thing is I went through a long battle with what I can now say was depression to step out of those shoes. I realize the painted on smile was not working anymore. I was sad all the time, I was ill towards the people I cared about and even more, I didn't have a desire to do the one thing I loved more than anything else –take care of my family. I was running out of steam and more, I was running out of hope.

It was at the point of complete and total burnout that I finally understood the statement: "You can lead a horse to water but you can't make it drink." My grandmother used to tell me that all the time. Now that she is gone to be with the Heavenly Father, I will admit I believed that if the horse was thirsty enough he would drink. Well that is true but it's not our responsibility to make the horse thirsty or force it to drink.

I felt by sacrificing my own happiness for someone else's I would be able to get what I needed from them. If I provided for their needs, or what I thought was their needs, they would in return provide or at least recognize my needs. It took a lot of years and even more soul searching to find out that people are going to do what they want to do, when they want to do it. Understand you cannot make anyone do anything. Yes, you can suggest. Yes, you can encourage. Yes, you can instruct. You can even put the ultimatum out there, but it is ultimately their choice as to what they want to do.

Unable to find my own happiness and realizing I could not make people cater to helping me find it, I was lost and unsure of what my next step would be. I felt trapped and confused. I had always put the needs of others before my own and now that was not working. My thoughts were truly if I can make this person just a little happier, my life would be better. I soon realized I was dressing from the inside out. I was hoping that doing something on the outside would help the inside and I was wrong.

So many of us are more concerned with how things look on the outside that we ignore what is on the inside. We focus our attention on what other people see and disregard what we see ourselves. We must stop dressing from the outside inward but dress from the inside outward. I was accustomed to satisfying the needs of everyone else, thinking that I was satisfying my own needs. I had dressed from the outside inward for so long that it appeared right to me.

I realized there would always be an opportunity to try to satisfy others. There would always be an opportunity to help one more person. There will always be an opportunity to say yes to one more demand even when you do not want to. When you begin to resent the things you are doing or when the things you once loved to do no longer feel good, it's time to look at the reason why you are doing them. So many times I felt that if I would just push a little more everything would be okay. In reality it was when I stopped pushing and began to look inside myself that it clicked. I wanted everyone around me to be thirsty because I was thirsty. Actually, I was dehydrated. I was at the point of death and didn't even know it. I was so consumed with making sure that everyone around me had water that I failed to take a drink for myself.

One day I looked in the mirror, making sure I was properly dressed and ready to greet the world. The image that stared back at me was unrecognizable. I had made a special effort to present myself as the "strong, loving woman" that everyone desired me to be, yet the person that stared back at me appeared to be weak and unlovable. Her eyes were sad. She looked tired and worn out. She looked defeated. I wanted to be what everyone else wanted me to be so bad that I stopped taking care of the person behind the clothes. It was at that moment that I fell on my knees and sobbed. I was tired of being tired. I was tired of putting on the charade like everything was okay. Being in that humble position forced me to understand I had to look inside to find what I really needed and ask God to help me with those needs.

I began to release others to be who they wanted to be and allowed them to lead their own lives. I then realized it freed up my energy and allowed me to be who I wanted to be. Soon, I had the strength to start working on those needs and my dreams began to come forth. As I began to love myself, my mother became one of my best friends, my children rose and called me blessed, my true friends accepted me as I was and not for what I could give them, and my husband returned, seeking to rectify the relationship that he walked away from.

My moment of truth was looking at my reflection in the mirror. What will it take for you? There must come a point when you get tired of living a mediocre life and realize there is more out there for you. It is at that moment that you have to reach up and ask God for help. I would be a liar if I said that moment changed me completely. I had moments when I slipped back into the habit of putting everyone's needs before my own. I remember one day sitting on my bed; it had been a very stressful month, and it seemed that nothing I did was enough. This particular night, I began to feel a tingling in my fingers. Soon the tingling stopped but I realized numbness had set in and it was gradually moving up the left side of my body. Within a matter of hours, my entire left side was numb and I could not move it. I was terrified. It was in the wee hours of the night and I did not want to alarm anyone. My kids were asleep and at the time, I was the only one in the house that could drive. I began to ask God to just allow me to make it to morning. I did not want to go to sleep, afraid my kids would awaken and find me dead. That was not an image I wanted for them. As I lay quietly in bed, time seemed to creep by. Finally I heard movement in the house; the kids were up preparing for school. Each morning I would pray with them before they left for the bus stop. This morning would be no different. I remember my son coming into the room and me making a joke saying for him to lift my hand because I was tired. The truth is, by this time I had no feeling and I could not lift it. We prayed and the older kids went off to the bus stop. I called for my youngest to get up and prepare for school. While he was in the bathroom, I forced myself to slide out of the bed towards the stairs. It took every bit of energy I had but I slid down each step until I made it to the bottom and sat there long enough to compose myself. Once he was ready I dragged myself to the car, drove him to school and then drove myself to the doctor. Once I arrived, the doctor informed me I was having symptoms of a stroke. As the tears ran down my face, I began to cry out to God. This was not possible. I could not get sick. I didn't have time for this right now. I had too much to do. I was still concerned about everyone else in the midst of an episode that could have killed me. I finally realized enough was enough.

I could think of many things to blame for that moment; but it was my desire to be superwoman that put me in that position. It wasn't until I was forced to make a change that I made one. I desire that you don't have to experience anything like that to realize that your happiness is in your hands. I truly believe we are in control of our destiny; we just have to know what we want and how to go after what we want.

Apply It

Write in your journal about what you really want or need right now. I could be love, attention, or acceptance, whatever you desire. Now ask yourself if you have ever said yes to a request not because you wanted to, but because you wanted your needs to be met by someone else and believed that if you accepted their request you would get it. Now write a letter of forgiveness to yourself for not seeking a way to fulfill that need yourself. Go back to the item or list of needs that you wrote in your journal and take the time to give them to yourself. You are capable of loving yourself when no one else is there to do it.

Dear God,

Help me to realize that when I say yes to things I really don't want to do, it is no longer an act of kindness, it is a yolk. Your word declares that You want me to have life and life more abundantly. You said You did not want me to live a life of bondage. You said I was your child and You want me healthy. Father, I am sorry for taking matters into my own hands and making them what I needed them to be instead of what you wanted them to be. Give me the strength to identify the needs that I have and help me to realize that You are the only One who can truly satisfy them. In Jesus' Name I pray. Amen.

Carry Your Own Cross

> *"We have no right to ask when sorrow comes, "Why did this happen to me?" unless we ask the same question for every moment of happiness that comes our way."* ~Author Unknown
>
> *"Obstacles are those frightful things you see when you take your eyes off your goal."* ~Henry Ford

My desire to bring the best out of people became an obsession to me. I would tackle any obstacle to help someone see the best in themselves. The problem was, I wasn't able to put the same effort in bringing the best out of myself. I couldn't see my own worth. I didn't know how to treat myself with love and respect which prompted individuals to not treat me with love or respect.

At this point in my life I can give this method of madness a name. I call it "carrying your own cross." I was so caught up in the desire to help other people carry their cross that I had forgotten to bring my own cross. When I reached the point that I needed a cross to bridge a gap that had formed, I also realized I had left my cross and was walking through life with someone else's on my back. The sad thing is it wasn't because they had given it to me to carry, it was because I decided that I needed to carry it. I needed to be part of their burden; I needed to be in control. They were not capable of going through their own trials, they needed my help. Mother don't cry, it will be okay; son or daughter it's okay if you make bad decisions that can ultimately destroy your life when you are older, mom will fix it; friends, I'm already taking care of five kids, a husband, working a full-time job, and in charge of this event but I can listen to your problems and solve them for you. Husband, I will stay up late and work on that presentation for you, and I will take care of all the household obligations while you enjoy your quiet time. I will turn my back when I need love and affection and you just don't have the time to give it to me because of your hectic schedule. I love you all so much and I realize you need ME to make your world complete. I love you so much that I will take all my energy and strength and bear all of your burdens because God did not equip you for the task like He has equipped me. I am superwoman.

Now that's funny! What in the world was I thinking? That's the problem - I wasn't thinking, I was reacting. I wanted so desperately to be in control of everything, that I laid my own cross down –the things I could control- and picked up what was not mine to begin with. Then when put in a situation where I needed my cross to continue my journey, I was forced to go back and pick it up. Not only was it a long and painful journey, every now and then I would find myself looking back at my family and friends and see them struggling to cross another bridge without my help. I so wanted to help them and many times I would run back to pick up the cross they had dropped only to have to start marching again to pick up my own. When I finally reached my cross and turned around many of those people that I had worked so hard to help were gone. They had vanished in the dark. They had moved on and started carrying their cross themselves or found someone else to carry it for them. The hurtful thing is - they were gone.

I did not feel I had anyone there who could help me carry my cross when I needed the assistance. I felt that no one understood the burdens associated with my cross. No one was strong enough to handle the issues surrounding my life. The road ahead seemed dark and lonely, but I knew I had to keep on going. I had a long road and a lot of territory to cover. The odd thing was, in this journey, I passed obstacles that I had already experienced while helping others, so passing those obstacles didn't take as much out of me. It was those hurdles that I had avoided for so long that gave me the battle of my life. I had to learn to accept that everyone would not like me. I had to learn that I could not be everything for everyone. I had to learn that I could not depend on someone else for my happiness. I had to learn there were life lessons that I had to achieve on my own. I am, however, grateful that God is gracious and provided many avenues of assistance - even encouragement when I wanted to give up.

There were people I passed along the way that I so urgently wanted to help but realized that I could not carry the load for them because that meant once again I would have to drop my own. As I walked down the street I can remember being at that point before. It made me so sad realizing if I had only brought my own cross with me the first time, I would not have to go through this painful event again. But as I tackled the road ahead, events that had once been full of excruciating pain were now bearable. God was building my strength and my self-confidence. He was molding me into who He had destined for me to be the whole time and I was letting Him. No longer did I fear not being loved, accepted or used. For the first time I was happy. I was walking along my path, with my cross on my shoulders and whistling. When trials came I would 'look up' to God and say, "Okay Daddy, now what should I do?" and it felt good.

I never want to give the impression that things were grand after going back and retrieving my cross. I was addicted to helping others. I truly felt that everyone needed my help and they would not be able to function in life without me. I was completely and totally delusional. My kids could not make it through life's challenges without me telling them what to do or what not to do. I felt my friends still needed my advice on how to raise their children or which hairdo looked better on them. My mother still needed me to do everything right to make her feel as if she had been successful in her child-rearing. And oh yes, my husband still needed me to remind him to take care of himself. It has been difficult to keep my hand out of the cookie jar but with God's help I'm working through the process.

The task was so difficult I found I had to use reverse psychology on myself. I believe there is a small child inside of all of us and if they don't receive the attention and love they need they will have temper tantrums. My inner child was yelling and screaming to the top of her lungs. She wanted to be loved. I continued learning how to nurture her and stand up for her. I began to make demands for her benefit-ultimately it was demands from me. No longer would I be made to feel that I did not deserve to be treated fairly. No longer would I settle for second best. This child deserved the best.

My children have always been my first priority. I could go without in order for them to have everything they needed in life, even if it was the things I felt they needed and they hadn't asked for. Remember I had to be in control even to the point of knowing what someone needed before they asked.

God has a way of turning even those "issues" you have into things He can use to help you see things His way. He took the obsession that I had of making someone else feel good and used it in my favor. I began to cater to that inner child. I began to listen to her. I began to spend time with her. I began to like her. I began to love her. I began to give her what she wanted before she could have an opportunity to ask. I was determined to save this child. She had been through so much hurt and pain – it was time for her to enjoy the benefits of being loved and I was the only one who could do it for her.

I began taking time to be by myself and listen to the calmness around me. I began to say no when I really wanted to. I began to allow people to show me the love that I desired. I began to accept the person I saw in the mirror without ridicule or pointing out everything wrong with her. I began to accept that I was not perfect. I began to accept that it was okay not to be. I began to accept that every day was not going to be full of roses. I began to accept the raindrops and expect the flowers would eventually come. I began to realize that people would treat me the way I allowed them to treat me and more importantly the way I treated myself. I realized I was a work in progress but each day I was getting closer to what God wanted me to be.

I can remember one thing that helped me to accept me as I was and to love me as I am. I sat down and wrote a letter of love to myself. I spoke of the things about me that I liked, the things I loved, the things I had accomplished and the things I was grateful for. It helped me to see that no longer did I have to focus on the negatives in my life. No longer did I have to accept what others said about me. No longer did I have to take the opinion of other people to justify or clarify who I am. I began to make a point of finding at least one thing each day that I was proud of about myself, one thing that I could feel good about. Every day was not easy. There were days that I had to pull out that letter and remind myself of my good qualities. I began to write affirmations about what God says about me and post them all over the mirror of my bathroom. I stopped allowing others to speak negativity into my life. If you didn't have something positive to say I would stop you in mid-sentence. Learning to carry my own cross and work towards building confidence in myself was a struggle. It continues to be a daily struggle, but it has been worth it.

Apply It

Look around your home and find an area that you can claim as yours. Now decorate it in a way that signifies who you are. It could be something as simple as removing everything that belongs to someone else from that area and replacing it with things that are important to you. This will be the area you will go to when you feel a need to retreat from life and turn your focus to that inner child. She needs you.

Dear God,
Thank You for this journey called life. Thank You for every hurdle. Thank You for the passion You have given me to want to help others. But Father now I need You to help me focus my attention on what You wanted me to learn during the most difficult times in my life. I do not want to dwell on them I want to learn from them. I want You to help me to realize how I have grown through each of them. In Jesus' Name I pray.

Dear God,
As I look inside myself and search for that inner child, give me the strength to love and nurture her. Give me the strength to move forward and to realize that every day I am a work in progress. I know that You love me in a way that no one else can. Now help me to see the qualities in myself that You see. Then help me to embrace them and strive to be all that You want me to be. Help me to realize that I am not responsible for carrying the cross of others. Help me to realize You have equipped them with everything they need to be successful and that the best way for me to be of assistance is to live a life that they can pattern. In Jesus' Name I pray.

The Strength to Let Go

> *"Don't cry when the sun is gone, because the tears won't let you see the stars."* ~Violeta Parra
>
> *"We must be willing to get rid of the life we've planned, so as to have the life that is waiting for us."* ~Joseph Campbell

When I look back over my life – hey isn't that a song? God has been right there with me. He never left me. He never forsook me. He was watching over me the whole time. It was I who pushed Him away. I was mad at Him. I was so wound up in self-pity and self-doubt that I walked away from the one and only being that could help me get back on my feet and onto solid ground. I had to realize that God and God alone was the only one who could bring me back to a state of sanity. He created me, He knows what I need, and more importantly He knows what I don't need.

I can remember being so angry with God. I remember saying to Him "I am your child. Everything you asked me to do I did it. How can you allow me to be hurt like this? If you love me take me out of my misery". Oh –yeah I was mad, no, I was hurt. I was lonely and I was in complete depression and didn't even realize it. I was walking around in denial. I thank God that He didn't listen to me and that He did love me so much that He delivered me.

It was at the end of that hopeless, helpless state of mind that it happened. At the point where I had completely hit rock bottom, I quit my job, my marriage was in disarray, my kids were angry, my house was a mess, and my heart was heavy. It was then that I looked up and said, "God, Daddy – I need your help I cannot do this anymore. I am hurting." It was then that He reached down and grabbed my hand. Then He took me in His arms and held me tight. It was then that for the first time in a very long time I began to feel comfort and strength. It was also then that I realized God had never left me. I had walked away from Him. I was so consumed with my hurt and pain that I had left the one Who could remove it.

Growing up in the church, I believed that God would speak through His servants and provide words of prophecy and confirmation to others. But I never thought it would happen to me. One night during a revival one of the visiting ministers called me to the front and asked if she could pray for me. Of course I said "yes". After the prayer she told me God wanted to use me in a mighty way but I was like a bag lady. I was walking around with layers upon layers of hurt and God was going to release me from it. She stated that when the layers began to shed everyone would be amazed at who I really was, including myself. Now this was at a time in my life where I felt everything was going pretty well and I was doing just fine. I could not imagine what she could be talking about. However, as time went on I began to feel the layers come off and the strength come upon me.

I began to realize that I was so consumed with being in control of the lives of others because I didn't want to deal with my own life. I didn't want to admit that I was a mess. I didn't want to acknowledge any of the layers of hurt that I had on my back. If I looked at the pieces of my own life I would have to admit failure. But that wasn't so. I sat down and had a long look at myself and realized some things about myself. I was strong. I was smart. I was a good mother. I was a good daughter. I was a good wife. I was a good person. I realized that I had choices. I realized that I had strength. The enemy had a desire to destroy me. I had buried all my pain and hoped that no one would see it. I hoped that eventually it would disappear, however I soon realized that true victory comes when you acknowledge that hurt and pain, get the help you need to overcome it, and then use that knowledge to help others. God had not designed me to be mistreated or abused. He had placed a calling on my life and through the layers of pain and hurt that I had endured, I would be able to grow into the person I needed to be.

The hardest part of my deliverance was letting go. As I have already told you I had a beautiful image of the way my life was supposed to be, the way things should be right now and would take place in the future. One thing I learned through all of this is there is no 'should-bes', no 'could-bes', and definitely no 'supposed-to-bes'. God's ways are not our ways and He knows what's best for us at all times.

Letting go was still very difficult, but it had to be done. I was holding on so tight that I felt I was losing my grip and this had to stop. All my life I was the one who felt the need to make everything perfect. I had to be the one to fix it if it was broken. Everyone looked to me to make sure it was done correctly.

What I realized was fixing everyone else's problems and making everyone else's lives perfect was making mine ragged and in complete turmoil. How do you let go when you've been doing this all your life? I'll tell you how -one day at a time.

I remember when my son was a baby - he was attached to his pacifier. He took it everywhere he went. He didn't really suck on it; he just held it in his mouth. I remember one day he wanted a cookie but didn't want to take the pacifier out of his mouth. I informed him that he could not have both. He cried and tried desperately to put both in his mouth. I can now see how God was showing me myself in that situation. I wanted to be free but didn't want to let go of the things that I felt comfortable with.

It seems that after that original word of prophecy was given to me more followed; each one with a more specific message and more clarity. I was told I needed to cut the strings that keep me bound. I prayed and asked God what strings He would require that I cut. By beginning to make an inventory of my life and what I desired in my life I was able to see things about me that were not Godly and things I didn't like. My desire to make everything perfect had become an obsession and controlled every part of my being. As I looked carefully at those areas in my life that I was obsessed with controlling, those areas I felt I had to hold on to, the areas I had to fix, I realized that I could not fix them – they were not for me to fix. I could not change how people acted or how they felt. I had to turn those matters over to God and cut the strings that were keeping me bound to them. As I examined those areas in my life that I had neglected by being so consumed with the "neglected" areas in lives of other people, I asked God to help me change the one thing I could change -- ME. I told you it was not an easy process.

Letting go was not easy and there are days I find myself wanting to grab hold of the strings, and tell someone what to do or analyze how they feel without asking them. It's at those times that I begin to feel drained and lonely and out of control and I stop and put focus where it belongs: on me and my own feelings. What did I need? What am I trying to avoid in my own life? What am I covering up? I had to cut these strings once and for all. As I began to cut the strings of bondage, I realized it was my grip on the strings that held me captive, not the strings themselves.

I had to learn that I could not control how people felt, neither what people did nor how they acted. I could not make them into what I wanted them to be. Only God could change them and He would make them into what He wants them to be in His own timing.

Once I finally learned I didn't have to control everything, people began to stand up and make their own decisions and learn to deal with the consequences of those choices. My obsession to make sure everything went smoothly had handicapped those individuals that I loved the most but more importantly put shackles on me that were hard to remove.

I also learned during that period of letting go, I had looked for man to be my provider, protector, and priest. I looked for man to make me feel good about myself. I looked to man to make me feel complete. In essence God is the only one who can provide that type of fulfillment. When you really let go you will realize there are people that come into your life for many different reasons. You have to be careful and only allow those individuals who desire to add value to you to stay. It's okay to detach yourself from people who desire to bring you down. I have always told people never to regret anything that once made you smile because it has contributed to who you are. However, if you find yourself always crying after events with the same person – it's time to cut them loose and ask God to send someone who will add wealth to your life. Many times you just need to allow Him to fulfill you in those areas. He's willing and more than able.

When I was finally able to accept that it wasn't my picture that mattered – that God was the holder of the blueprint of my life, I began to loosen my grip. I began to accept things as they were. I began to ride the wave of life and enjoy each splash of water on my face. All my life I hid behind other people's issues in order not to have to deal with my own. I was good at pointing out what someone else was doing wrong but could never quite see what I was doing wrong. It was when I stopped focusing on everyone else and attacked my own issues head on that I was able to let go and allow God to take control of my life.

I was able to forgive all the hurtful things that were said and done to me over the years. I was able to articulate what I needed. I was able to set boundaries against those things and people who spoke negatively into my life. I was able to shut off the recorder in my mind that highlighted the flaws of what I saw when I looked in the mirror. I was able to breathe. I was able to live. My creativity returned. My hope returned. My sense of purpose was made clear. We've all heard the expression "if I knew then what I know now things would be different." Well I'm glad I didn't know then what I know now. There are too many things in my life that would have been missing if I had not experienced my waves of life. What I have learned is to be grateful for every aspect, every component, every issue, and every moment because it has strengthened me and made me look within for the strength that has always been there; I just didn't know it.

Apply It

What has God allowed you to go through in life that can be used to help someone else? Think about a time in your life where you needed someone to speak life into a dead situation. Now think of someone you can do something kind for. There are women's shelters, orphanages, babies that need to be held in a nursery. Schedule a day to show love to someone outside of your circle. Write in your journal how this act of kindness made you feel.

Dear God,
You have given me talents and I have dug a hole and buried them, either out of fear or because I didn't see a need to use them. I ask that You will help me to uncover those talents and use them to edify You. I ask that You help me to use the obstacles in my life to grow and help someone else. I know that You love me and desire for me to have a full life and that You have equipped me with everything I need to do just that. As I journey to make an impact in someone else's life, help me to remember the impact that You are making on mine right now. Help me to see that my strength is directly connected to You. In Jesus' Name I pray.

Loving Me Is Okay

> "Nobody can go back and start a new beginning but anyone can start today and make a new ending." ~ Maria Robinson
>
> "When life takes the wind out of your sails, it is to test you at the oars." ~Robert Brault

When I was able to stop worrying (yes worrying) so much about what everyone else was doing or wasn't doing and stop trying to fix everyone else's issues I began to fix what was going on in my life. I began to look inside to see what I needed to be happy. I began to reveal the real me not to the world but to myself. I began to stop hiding behind the things that happened in my past and realized the blessings in them.

The prophecy of being a bag lady reared its ugly head once again. I was walking around with layers upon layers of hurt and guilt and I needed God to remove them. As He began to work, what came forth amazed me.

I always saw myself as a weak and needy person. I saw myself as needing a man to complete me. I saw myself as a failure unable to complete tasks that were placed before me. But as the layers began to come off so did all the negative images that I had of myself. I realized I had jumped every hurdle that came forth in life. I began to accept that each obstacle that was placed before me was to prepare me for this point in my life. God has placed a burning inside of me to use my life's story to help those who are hurting, those who are at a point of wanting to give up. He has helped me realize that the hurt and shame that I was feeling was a trick from the enemy so that others would not be helped by what I went through. He helped me to realize that it is all in His timing and that all I'm required to do is to love myself the way He loves me, to be patient with myself the way He is patient with me and to love others as He has loved me.

I became more patient with myself and realized that I don't have to be perfect. God does not require that of me. I learned that every lesson I am to learn will be learned when God deems I am ready for it. I have learned that not only am I a strong person, I am a lovable person that deserves to be loved. It feels good to look in the mirror and love who I see. No longer do I obsess about whether my hair is in place, or that my clothes are up with the latest fashion. I don't worry about those things because they are superficial. I don't worry if people will see the hurt in my eyes or the fear in my heart because the hurt and fear is gone. I don't worry about whether my kids will be accepted amongst their peers for I realize that as long as they are acceptable to God that's all that matters.

I never want to give the impression that all is well every day. I do however, want to let you understand that I have accepted the fact that it's okay. If I reach down and grab hold to the strings of bondage, if I look in the mirror and those negative recordings begin to play, if that lonely feeling or insecurity arises within me, I know that I can pray and ask God to help me and He is faithful to provide my every need. When you are able to love yourself the way that God loves you, everything else falls into place and the small stuff doesn't matter.

We are all going through the same thing, just on a different level. When I first heard that statement, I did not believe it but as I conclude what was the most difficult season of my life, I realize it is true. We are all a work in progress, trying to figure out where we fit in this world and in God's plan. Whether we are a teenager, a single adult, an experienced married adult or a widower, we all must take the time to see ourselves as God sees us and take time to love the person within. We must remember that God will never forsake us. He will always be right there carrying us through the rough and tough areas. As you take a moment to reflect on all the things in your life that got you down, those things that seemed to have destroyed a part of who you are, remember we are all going through. But that's the point of it all, in order to get to the other side you must go through something.

Apply It

Write a letter of thanksgiving to acknowledge every obstacle, every hurdle, every situation you deemed bad. Then give thanks for the opportunity to be able to look back on them and see that you made it through. Now breathe in that victory and realize it's okay.

Dear God,

Thank you so much for each obstacle, trial, and hurdle that has been placed in my life. I realize that those situations have made me who I am and will draw me closer to you. Father, help me to not bury the pain anymore. Help me to see the triumph in what I have accomplished. In Jesus' Name I pray. Amen.

Just a Little Better

> "God brings men into deep waters, not to drown them, but to cleanse them." ~John Aughey

> "Man performs and engenders so much more than he can or should have to bear. That's how he finds that he can bear anything." ~William Faulkner

My prayer is that you are a step closer to loving yourself, forgiving others, accepting who you are and what you have gone through as a source of growth. I hope you remember that some of those things in life that we work so hard to nurture are the things that God wants to pluck away to make us who He wants us to be. My prayer is that my story of trials and self-awareness has helped you realize that you are not alone, we are all going through, just on a different level.

I pray you understand that God is faithful and He loves you. He is standing with His arms wide open, waiting for you to accept His love. Life can be extremely hard, especially when you don't know your own purpose and you have such a desire to please others. You cannot change anyone. You cannot fix everything. You do not have to be perfect. You have to be loved. You deserve to be loved. You deserve to be accepted. You deserve to have hope and to dream. But you have to remember that it all starts with you. People will treat you the way you treat yourself. If you want them to see you as a strong person, you must see yourself as a strong person. If you want others to believe in your dreams, you must believe in your dreams.

Your life is a borrowed instrument from God. If you were to let your neighbor borrow one of your possessions, you would expect them to return it in the same condition or better than when they got it from you. You are one of God's most prized possessions. He created you in His image. He wanted you to have the abundance of life. He wants only the best for us, yet we allow people to mistreat us, use us and we find ways to make it our fault. We come back to God broken, dirty and worn out, but thankfully He loves us so much that He's just glad that we returned.

Everyone should set goals for themselves. You should always strive to be a little better. Walking in your destiny can only be accomplished one step at a time. But in order to walk in that destiny you have to keep walking. Many times I have found myself right at the finish line and allowed fear to overtake me. What I realize now, is that for me to cross the finish line whether it be running, walking, or crawling – I have to cross it. It's my way of returning God's possession back to Him just a little better.

ABOUT THE AUTHOR

Author Tina Bailey is a wife and mother who empowers people daily through words of encouragement, support, and prayer. Tina especially enjoys ministering to women's groups by sharing her uplifting messages of God's love and acceptance. She resides in Cary, North Carolina with her family where she owns and operates "Gifts by Tina," a custom gift service.

Book Order Form

To order copies of this book, indicate the number of copies you would like next to the title, provide your shipping address and contact information, enclose payment including shipping, and mail this form to:

Tina Bailey/Rain Publishing
PO Box 702
Knightdale, NC 27545

What You're Hiding is Hindering Your Blessings
@$11.99 each   X _____

Shipping and Handling: $5.00
Total Enclosed: _____

Shipping Address:

Name: _____

Street: _____

City, State, Zip_____

Phone: _____

Email: _____

www.ingramcontent.com/pod-product-compliance
Lightning Source LLC
Chambersburg PA
CBHW072058290426
44110CB00014B/1738